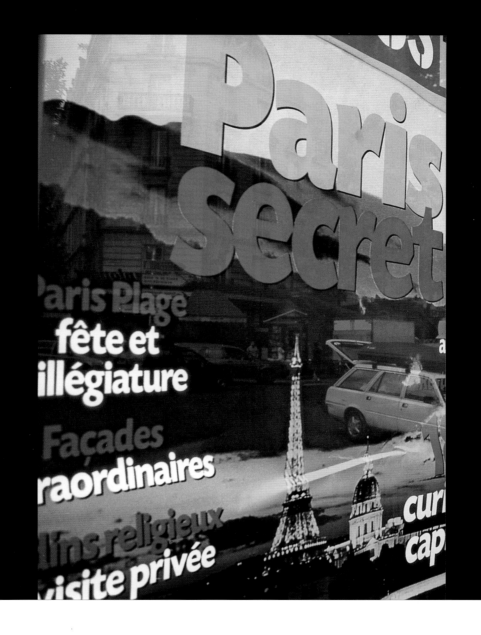

Paris

CITY OF LIGHT AND FASCINATION

THUNDER BAY
P · R · E · S · S
San Diego, California

TEXT
GUY PIERRE BENNET

EDITORIAL PROJECT
Valeria Manferto De Fabianis

GRAPHIC DESIGN
Clara Zanotti

GRAPHIC REALIZATION
Clara Zanotti
Patrizia Balocco Lovisetti

EDITORIAL COORDINATION
Giada Francia
Federica Romagnoli
Enrico Lavagno

7 LEFT A café in Montmartre. In the old quarters of the city, the nostalgic revival of the past is not at all artificial. Everyone knows that in Paris, elegance and sophistication are completely natural.

7 RIGHT A fountain in Place Stravinsky in Beaubourg. As if to confirm the timelessness of Parisian charm, the vertiginous neatness of the Gothic and the shining, unbridled imagination of the work by Niki de Saint Phalle and Jean Tinguely confront each other in the setting of the *centre ville* of Paris, a few steps from the Ile de la Cité.

CONTENTS

INTRODUCTION

PARIS, THE CAPTIVATING CITY OF LIGHTS

Paris is a city that is always at the center of our desires and our interest.

It is a unique city, throbbing with images and emotions, the symbol of an art of living, an art of loving. A city where sounds, colors, smells, and memories echo each other. They intertwine. Sometimes they blur together. Sometimes they fight each other. Paris, city of illusions and mirages, of laughter and tears, is always different for each of us, depending on how much of ourselves we've left there. This book is not a photographic inventory of the usual "hallowed" places—Paris has been photographed time and time again. And it's not a city that gives itself up easily to just anybody. Only those who are in love with Paris can discover its soul, discover that under the surface there are things capable of inspiring the deepest emotions. This book is an invitation to dream, an invitation to go on a timeless journey through the imagery of collective memory, to go on aesthetic and personal sentimental adventures.

A Paris that is intimate but not secret.

A Paris that is sparkling but not vulgar.

A Paris that is spectacular but not contrived.

A Paris that is sentimental but not sugary.

Here, Paris shakes off its traditional decorative function and shows itself for what it really is, a unique city where the wind of inspiration, spirit, and emotion blows. For this to happen, we have to look at Paris with our eyes, but see it with our hearts.

And since the charm and the poetry of Paris is impossible to explain, we wanted to act as though we'd created it ourselves.

Above all, do not expect this book to be something it's not.

To hell with precise information, useful for visitors.

To hell with the trendiest bars and clubs, the "unmissable" sightseeing, the opening times of the museums, the historical tours. That is not the purpose of this book. Here is a Paris for travelers who are sensitive to the atmosphere and seduction of places and words.

A Paris made up of moments stolen from passing time.

A Paris where one can find, simply, a fragment of pleasure and beauty.

PARIS VIVANT

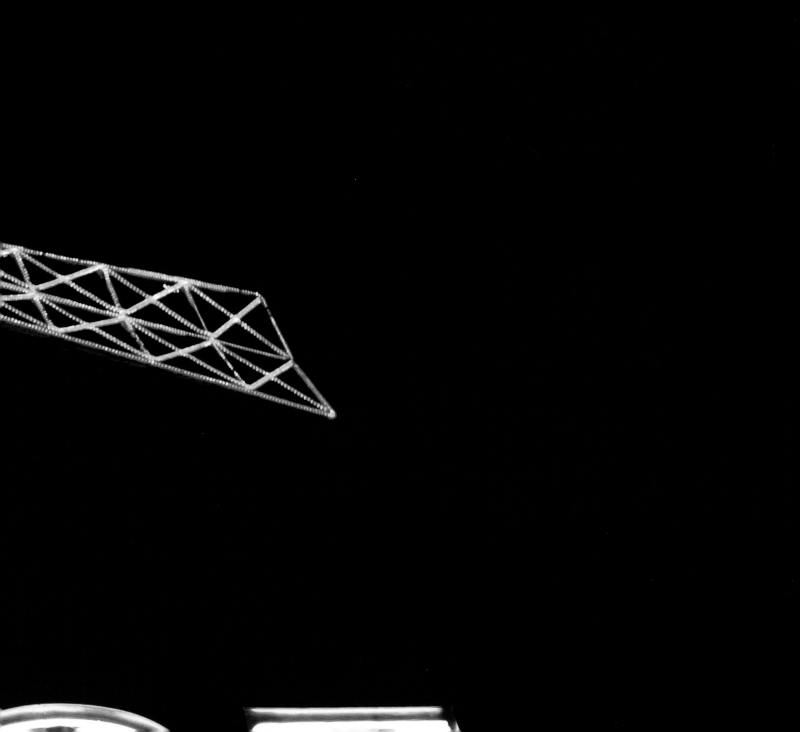

PARIS IN CENTURIES

FOLIES-BERGÈRE

16 FROM LEFT TO RIGHT LOUIS XIV, THE SUN KING, IN A PORTRAIT DONE BY HYACINTHE RIGAUD IN 1701; NAPOLEON BONAPARTE VISITING THE LOUVRE IN 1805; A POSTER ADVERTISING THE THÉATRE DES FOLIES BERGÈRE, THE OLDEST MUSIC HALL IN PARIS; JUNE 1939: THE WEHRMACHT PARADES DOWN THE CHAMPS ELYSÉES, AT THE FOOT OF THE ARC DE TRIOMPHE.

17 THE EIFFEL TOWER BECAME THE QUINTESSENTIAL SYMBOL OF THE "NEW PARIS" THAT WAS BEING CREATED AT THE CHAMP-DE-MARS. THE STRUCTURE, WHICH HAD BEEN RECENTLY COMPLETED, TOWERED OVER THE PAVILIONS AT THE 1889 INTERNATIONAL EXPOSITION. RISING TO A HEIGHT OF 985 FEET, IT WAS BUILT WITH 8,000 TONS OF STEEL.

18 VERCINGETORIX CALLED FOR A GALLIC UPRISING IN 52 BC. THE PARISII JOINED IN THE REVOLT AGAINST CAESAR, BUT VERCINGETORIX LOST THE BATTLE OF ALESIA AND WAS PUT TO DEATH BY THE ROMANS.

19 TOP THE FIRST MAP OF PARIS DATES FROM THE THIRD CENTURY BC, AT THE BEGINNING OF THE ROMAN OCCUPATION. YOU CAN SEE THE NATURAL SITE ON WHICH THE CITY WAS LATER BUILT.

19 BOTTOM THE FIRST GOLD COINS USED BY THE PARISII AT THE END OF THE SECOND CENTURY BC.

Paris is intimately connected to the Seine, the river that has shaped its appearance and lifestyle. Lutetia, the city of the Gauls, rose on the Île de la Cité, in the midst of that great stream of water, because it was a favorable place. In those days, clusters of small islands dotted the Seine, which was broader and shallower than it is today. They have now mostly disappeared, because they were gradually connected to the shores or to each other in order to create terra firma on which to build. The Seine and its tributaries are the means of communication that have made the economic development of the city possible since prehistoric times. During construction of the new quarter of Bercy, mechanical shovels recently turned up oak pirogues over five thousand years old.

Paris also had the good fortune to be located in the middle of a sedimentary basin from which builders could take the limestone, rocks, clay, and sand they needed to construct houses, bridges, and monuments.

But we can bet that the early inhabitants of the area, the Parisii, could not have imagined what would become of their village, built haphazardly amid unhealthy marshes regularly flooded by the river.

No one knows when the city took on the name by which we know it today. It is thought that this occurred sometime between the fifth and the sixth centuries. Neither does anyone know where its original name came from.

We do know that "Lutetia" is mentioned for the first time in Caesar's *De bello Gallico*, a description of his eight-year campaign in Gaul. In 53 BC, an assembly of Gauls met at Lutetia as Caesar, the dictator of Rome, was conquering Europe. The following year, the Parisians allied themselves with Vercingetorix—the first of a long list of national French heroes—who was defeated and executed at Alesia.

The Romans occupied Paris for three centuries, which, in the end, was not a misfortune. Builders of empires, the Quirite, or Roman, architects never tired of "civilizing" that modest village. They built markets, temples, public baths, bridges, comfortable dwellings, a circus, an aqueduct, and a grid of straight roads that delineated the quarters, this design strictly reflecting their military camps.

The first streets in Paris were the *cardo*, now rue Saint Jacques, which bisects the city from north to south leading to Orléans, and the *decumanus*, now rue Saint Martin, which, from west to east, crosses the Seine and runs as far as Soisson.

By the end of the Roman occupation, Paris had about eight thousand inhabitants.

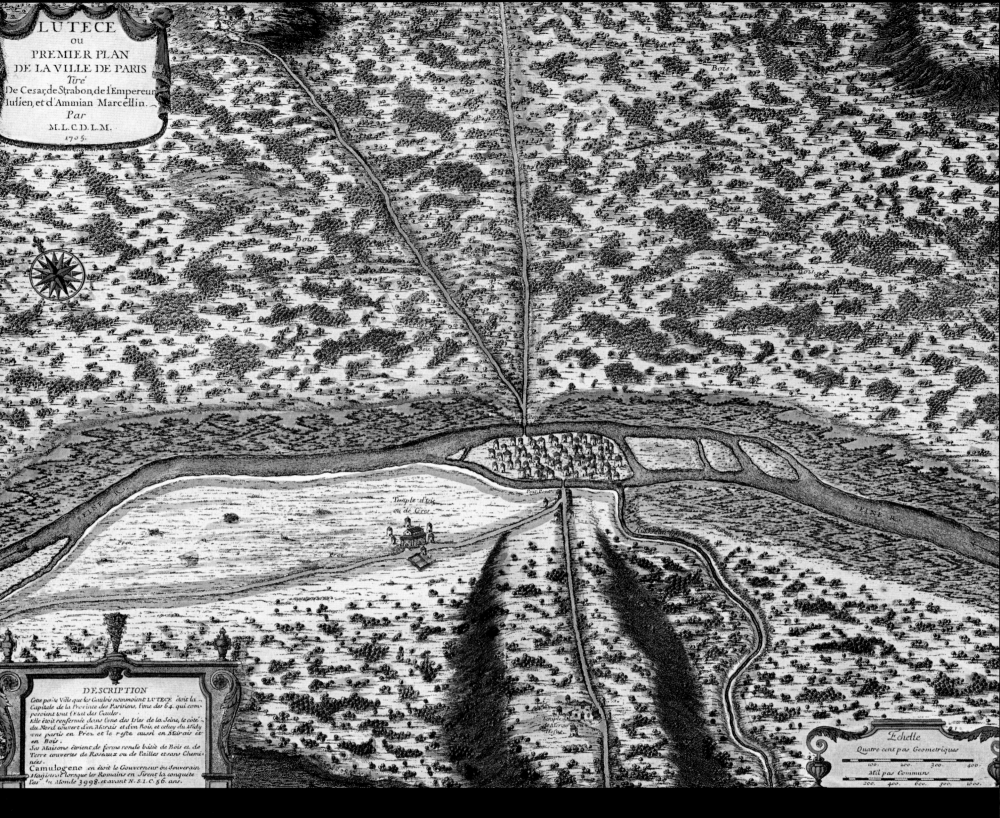

LUTECE
ou
PREMIER PLAN
DE LA VILLE DE PARIS
Tiré
De Cesar, de Strabon, de l'Empereur
Julien, et d'Ammian Marcellin.
Par
M. L. C. D. L. M.
1705.

Bois.

Bois.

Bois.

Bois.

Bois.

Bois.

Bois.

Bois.

SEINE.

SEINE.

Temple d'Isis
ou de Cerés.

Prez.

Prez.

Petit Pont.

Temple
de Mercure
ou d'Isis.

DESCRIPTION

Cete petite Ville que les Gaulois nommoient LUTECE étoit la
Capitale de la Province des Parisiens, l'une des 64. qui com-
posoient tout l'Etat des Gaules.
Elle étoit renfermée dans l'une des Isles de la Seine, le côté
du Nord couvert d'un Marais et d'un Bois, et celui du Midi
d'une partie en Prez et le reste aussi en Marais et
en Bois.
Ses Maisons étoient de forme ronde bâtie de Bois et de
Terre couvertes de Roseaux ou de Pailles et sans Chemi-
nées.
Camulogene en étoit le Gouverneur ou Souverain
Magistrat lorsque les Romains en firent la conquête
l'an du Monde 3998. et avant N. S. I. C. 56. ans.

Echelle
Quatre cent pas Geometriques
100.   200.   300.   400.
Mil pas Communs
200.   400.   600.   800.   1200.

CHRISTIAN PARIS: SAINTS AND KINGS

It took three centuries for Paris to awaken, centuries that bring us to the epoch of the barbarian invasions. The first invasions to touch the city were those of the Huns, led by Attila. At this time, Geneviève, a rich landowner from Nanterre, appeared on the scene. She consecrated her virginity to god, and brought herself fame through her numerous miracles, wonders that earned her the devotion of the people. In AD 451, when Attila was on the outskirts of Paris, she galvanized crowds and exhorted the people to defend themselves. The Huns, pushed back, attacked Orléans instead. Geneviève, raised to the altar, is now the patron saint of Paris and her name has been given to one of the liveliest quarters in the capital, a hill that the Parisians call "Montagne" Sainte Geneviève (the chronicles say she was nearly six feet tall and had the shoulders of a stevedore). Also through Geneviève, Christianity made its entrance into the city, and the first churches were implanted into the remaining Roman temples. Parisians, like Romans, have always had a strong ability to bounce back.

At the beginning of the sixth century, Clovis was the king of France. At Soisson, he expelled the last representatives of Roman authority and, with one blow of his club, cracked the skull of a soldier who had had the audacity to break a vase that he liked. This anecdote is one of the most famous in French history.

In 508 Clovis installed himself in Paris, making it the capital of a kingdom with borders that fluctuated according to the wars being fought.

The Merovingian era began. The city covered itself with churches—the most famous, a modest structure built on the Île de la Cité and dedicated to Saint Etienne, would become the Cathedral of Notre Dame in the eleventh century. From the same period come the churches of Saint-Germain-des-Près and Saint-Denis, several times razed to the ground and rebuilt during the turmoil of the city's history.

Paris grew. It grew politically under the influence of the sons and successors of Clovis, Childebert I and especially Clotaire I, who in 561 declared Paris to be a Frankish city so that no pretender to the throne could enter. However, the growth of the city was mostly economic, due to the management of the clever Saint Eloi, who, at the beginning of the seventh century, promoted the development of goldsmiths' workshops. Paris became the European center for the production of gold coins that spread throughout not only Gaul but also in the Low Countries, England, Germany, and the Iberian peninsula. The city attracted foreigners, who went there for the first commercial fairs, endowing it with a fame that today still clings to it like a sheath—a silk one, obviously. Paris became renowned as the capital of luxury. Valuable fabrics, glass, ceramics, jewelry, spices, and even carved sepulchers—everything that was Parisian brought merchants from places as far off as Judea and Syria. The Palu market, at the entrance of the Petit-Pont, became the center of the bilateral trading of that era. Paris had, at that time, twenty thousand inhabitants.

SOISSONS

ORLEANS

PARIS

22 IN 886 NORMAN INVADERS ATTACKED PARIS, ATTEMPTING TO ENTER THE CITY THROUGH THE TOWER OF THE GRAND PONT. THEY WERE DRIVEN AWAY BY ODO, WHO WAS CROWNED KING IN 888.

23 HUGH CAPET WAS CROWNED IN 988, INAUGURATING THE THIRD DYNASTY OF FRENCH KINGS, THE CAPETIANS, WHO RULED UNTIL 1328.

CAROLINGIANS AND CAPETIANS

But, alas, Saint Eloi was not immortal and neither was the Merovingian power, which ended and was replaced by the Carolingians in the early seventh century. There followed a lineage of brilliant kings who did not feel the same enthusiasm for Paris as their predecessors had. Carloman moved his capital to Rome and Aix-la-Chapelle. Charles Martel and Pepin the Short limited themselves to sporadic visits to the city, though both decided to have themselves buried in the wealthy Abbey of Saint-Denis.

In short, abandoned by its kings, Paris declined. The minters went elsewhere to coin their money, the fairs were rare, and the Jews and Syrians went to the other side of the Rhine. The city then decided to shine with a new splendor, that of the arts and culture. Remi d'Auxerre, one of the great men of letters of that age, founded the first school in Paris that we know of, which probably was on the site where the Sorbonne is now found.

Paris was no longer just a city of beautiful ruins. It was beautiful enough, though, to attract the cupidity of the greedy. Those that stand out particularly were the Teutons, who roamed the surroundings of Paris like vultures, and the Normans, descendents of the Vikings, who fell upon the weakened capital coveting its supposed treasures. During the first half of the ninth century, Paris constantly faced the menace of these new invaders who, sailing up the Seine, devastated Burgundy and reached the capital, sacking it and setting it on fire several times, or saving it in exchange for considerable amounts of ransom.

In 886, the date of the last Norman expedition, Paris was bloodless, its churches almost entirely destroyed and its population decimated.

In 911, King Charles the Simple put an end to the Norman menace, giving the fearsome barbarians the regions west of Gaul, the area that later became Normandy.

When peace returned, the last of the Carolingians, who had allowed the invaders to sack and burn the city, were thrown out of the city and handed over to the military. It was Odo (also known as Eudes), Count of Paris and its exemplary defender, who had himself elected king, inaugurating the epoch of the Capetians. Finally, the Capetians, to whom Paris owes so much! This is especially true of their first representative, Hugh Capet, who first attracted attention to himself in the defense of the city, which Otto II of Germany was eyeing, by turning back the barbarian emperor beyond the borders of the Rhine. In 987 Hugh became king of France and entered triumphantly into Paris. A great politician who was enamored of his capital, he impelled the city to become once again the power center of the kingdom, and it expanded from the Île de la Citè to the Right Bank of the Seine. Capet quickly understood that the true wealth of Paris was the river. Through laws and edicts, he promoted the development of the guild of boatmen, whose corporation became the most powerful in the kingdom. It was so influential that it gave the city its coat of arms, a boat with its sails furled, voyaging in stormy waters, and its motto, *Fluctuat nec mergitur* (It is tossed by the waves but does not sink).

24 TOP NOTRE DAME DE PARIS WAS CONSTRUCTED BETWEEN 1163 AND 1250. IT WAS SACKED DURING THE REVOLUTION AND RESTORED BY VIOLET LEDUE, WHO ADDED ITS STEEPLE.

24 BOTTOM THE PALACE-FORTRESS OF THE LOUVRE (HERE SEEN AROUND 1360) WAS BUILT BY ORDER OF PHILIP AUGUSTUS IN 1190.

25 PHILIP II WAS THE FIRST KING OF FRANCE TO BEAR THAT TITLE. CROWNED IN 1180, THIS WARRIOR KING CONSIDERABLY CONSOLIDATED THE POWER OF THE CAPETIAN DYNASTY.

NOTRE DAME AND THE LOUVRE

For Paris, this was the beginning of a new commercial era. First, the Grand Marché moved from the Île de la Cité to an area called des Champeaux, quite far from the Seine. Renamed the Marché des Halles, it remained the heart of Paris until 1969 when, because of problems of space and traffic jams, it was moved to Rungis. Then, on the Right Bank, the market and port of Grève—now the square of City Hall—were created. In 1163, Bishop Maurice de Sully decided to build the Cathedral of Notre Dame on the site of the Church of Saint Etienne, which, for that age, was a work of unusual and audacious architecture and beauty. It is a miracle of balance that uses cross vaults and gives space to the light, letting it pour inside through immense windows. The construction of Notre Dame was an epic event which kept Parisians employed for two centuries with 160,000 workmen, architects, and artists of every kind who took turns at creating a masterpiece that was finished only at the beginning of the fourteenth century. "Paris would not be Paris without Notre Dame," wrote Victor Hugo. Indeed, the cathedral has been the site of some of the most important events in the life of the capital, including Napoleon proclaiming himself emperor, the beatification of Joan of Arc, and the first mass after the Liberation during which General Charles de Gaulle miraculously escaped an attempt on his life.

Over two centuries, the Capetians really made Paris the capital of the kingdom, giving new luster to its coat of arms. They built a royal palace on the Île de la Cité, restored or reconstructed the churches, and put up bridges across the Seine, among them the first one in stone, the Pont au Change, protected by scaffolds and watch towers. The old marshes were reclaimed and cultivated. After Philip Augustus came to power in 1180, he had the city renovated and the important streets paved. He built fountains fed by the waters of the Belleville stream and deviated the wastewater, which ran freely, toward an open-air sewer on the outskirts of the

city. He also set up a garbage collection system using the coastal inhabitants, who deposited it in delimited public dumps. That refuse, amassed over centuries, would become the hill that is occupied by the Parc des Buttes-Chaumont. Adjacent villages were connected to the city. New churches were built, such as Saint Paul and Saints Innocents. And the Capetians brought back the Jews and Syrians, who re-established trade with Europe.

In 1190, King Philip Augustus demanded that the bourgeoisie finance the construction of city walls capable of resisting the assaults of its enemies across the Channel. He also included a fort, the Louvre. Then, reassured, he went on a crusade.

In the eleventh century Paris was reputed to be impregnable and was famous as the most beautiful Christian city. The Île de la Cité was overpopulated, and the capital swept away the earliest city walls and crossed the Seine, expanding along the Right Bank. The Left Bank, on the other hand, evoked little interest among the builders and was left abandoned, divided from the city by a wall. Some vintners installed themselves there and began producing a light wine appreciated by the students who, to move closer to the producers, settled on the Left Bank, giving birth to the Latin Quarter. The settling of the Left Bank did not occur for just this simple reason. The teachers of the Parisian Episcopal schools, renowned throughout Europe, wanted to remove themselves from religious tutelage and create independent centers of study, which obviously did not have the approval of either the king or the bishop. The students revolted and won, installing themselves in the institute thanks to the intercession of Pope Innocent III, who had the best reasons for sowing discord between the king of France and his intellectual élite. The school was recognized in 1252 and received the right to have a seal. In 1257, a canon, Robert de Sorbon, the confessor of the king and a great man of learning, founded the school of theology that became the Sorbonne.

26 LEFT Legend has it that the canons of Notre Dame had to donate their beds to the ward upon their deaths.

26 RIGHT Right next to Notre Dame, the Hôtel Dieu is the oldest hospital in Paris. This refuge for the indigent was finally rebuilt in 1868.

27 Louis IX was one of the most famous kings in the history of France because he aided the poor and established order.

SAINT LOUIS

Philip Augustus was succeeded by his nephew Louis IX, better known as Saint Louis—the same Saint Louis who administered justice under the oak tree at Poissey and washed the feet of the poor. He was responsible for the building of Sainte Chapelle, a jewel of Gothic architecture, destined to host Christ's crown of thorns and some fragments of the true cross, ransomed for their weight in gold from the emperor of Byzantium. Good Saint Louis decided to live in the palace on the Île de la Citè, and the dignitaries of his court followed suit, building luxurious private palaces wherever a little space could be found. The houses of the people remained the usual tottering huts, each one supporting the other. Their ground floors were made of stone, while the three or four floors above were constructed of wood and of mortar composed of mud and straw, excellent attractions for the frequent fires that, when they occurred, were devastating. The dilapidated houses in compact lines bordered narrow alleys and were built everywhere, even on bridges and riversides up to the level of the water.

Business was flourishing. Shops were overflowing with marvelous goods from the four corners of the civilized world: wines from Burgundy, wood from Morvan, marble from Italy, ivory from Africa, cloth and brocades from Spain, blades from Toledo, linen from Holland, salt from Brittany, and more. One hundred and one different professional categories were recorded, divided into powerful guilds such as the water merchants and the butchers, who obeyed only the provosts of their corporations. The Lombards (Italian bankers mostly from Piedmont and Tuscany) and Jews controlled the circulation of gold. The Jews were forced to wear a *rouelle*, a round piece of cloth that set them apart from other Parisians, and, depending on the financial needs of the king, were regularly subjected to paying "generous" but obligatory taxes to fill the royal coffers.

Large hospitals were opened. The Hôtel Dieu took in the indigent, but the sanitary conditions were such that more patients died of infection than were cured. The Saint Lazare leprosarium catered especially to returning Crusaders, while the Quinze-Vingts, a hospital that took in three hundred blind people (fifteen times twenty, which explains the name of the institute), operated thanks to donations from the bourgeoisie eager to ingratiate themselves with the king.

Paris was growing and needed an enormous labor force, so workers trying their fate and fortune flooded in from the most distant provinces of the kingdom as well as from Austria, Italy, and Portugal. This was the beginning of the great waves of immigration that gave the city a reputation as a welcoming and tolerant place. Paris during the Middle Ages was an immense teeming market that had nearly three hundred thousand inhabitants, an astonishing figure for that period. Its political and commercial importance was at its height. It attracted intellectuals, scientists, and scholars from all over Europe who came to see it for themselves. It certainly was a glittering city: painters, sculptors, goldsmiths, embroiderers, glass makers, and brass workers created the successful luxury crafts while illusionists, acrobats, and jugglers offered astounding spectacles in church squares.

Broadly speaking, Paris included the Île de la Citè, the commercial city on the Right Bank, and the university quarter on the Left Bank, all within city walls that were reputed to be insurmountable. The Seine ran through the center and acted both as a means of transport and as an element of vital importance for the citizens of Paris. There the people drew water, fished, and bathed. The river made the grindstones of the mills turn; it transported barges full of merchandise; and it even served as a sewer and a grave. We can only imagine the degree of pollution: to ensure drinkable water, people dug wells down to the water tables, but even these wells were contaminated by infiltration of residue from slaughterhouses and tanneries. Many died of dysentery and other malignant fevers. Still, Parisians were clean: despite the poor quality of the water, in 1292 the city had thirty public baths heated by stoves.

28-29 In 1380, Paris was a city that had grown considerably along the Right Bank of the Seine.

29 LEFT Crowned in 1285, Philip IV was a great head of state. He is considered to be the first modern monarch.

29 RIGHT The Bastille, in its origins in 1370, was a fortress built to protect Paris. Later Richelieu made it a state prison. It was destroyed on July 14, 1789.

JOAN OF ARC AND THE HUNDRED YEARS' WAR

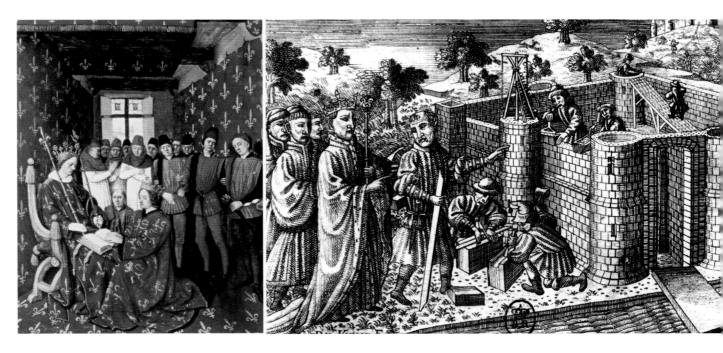

The last Capetian, Charles IV, died in 1328. The legitimate heir should have been Edward III, nephew of Philip of Valois, but there was a small problem: he was the king of England. The crown of France, therefore, came to Philip of Valois (the Fortunate), cousin of the deceased king, a decision that provoked the Hundred Years' War. Paris was gripped by torment and lived, for nearly a century and a half, at the mercy of terrible vicissitudes. The conflict against the English ruined business. The clans that aspired to the throne—the Burgundians and the Armagnacs—made the city an arena for their own ambitions. There was the civil war conducted by the Jacques, organized bands of peasants in revolt, as well as civil insurrections such as that of the Maillotins, who refused to pay the exorbitant taxes demanded by the provost and who greeted tax collectors with iron clubs.

Thus the period of famine and widespread epidemics arrived. In 1348, the Black Death, the Plague, hit Paris. Very soon cadavers blocked the streets. Pyres were improvised in the squares. The decades passed. It is said that between 1420 and 1440, wolves driven by hunger entered the city to feed upon babies.

Paris was the theater of disorderly popular uprisings and civil insurrections, organized sacking, extortion, political homicides, and summary executions. It lost half of its population. A large number of homes and shops were abandoned. Philip of Valois had tried to check the increase in crime, giving the city the Bastille, its first real prison. Among its most famous guests would be Louis XIV's superintendent of finance, Nicolas Fouquet, guilty of being richer than the king; the Man in the Iron Mask, the presumed twin of the Sun King; and the Marquis de Sade, the sulfurous eighteenth-century writer. The building itself, a symbol of royal absolutism, was destroyed by the populace in 1789, leaving an immense space, the preferred setting from then on, in which the joys and revolts of the capital have been expressed.

In 1422, Henry VI, at six months of age, was proclaimed the king of France and England, and a year later the English, who had won the war, triumphantly entered a humiliated Paris. The Duke of Bedford, uncle of Henry VI, named himself regent of the city and installed himself in the Hôtel des Tournelles.

It was at this time that Joan of Arc, the Maid of Orléans, heard divine voices that exhorted her to throw out the invaders. She forced Charles VII, the king of France in exile, to lay siege to Paris to have what was due to him by right. The siege failed. She tried again to rouse the sovereign but he preferred to wait in perfect tranquility for the Maid to keep her promise and push the English back across the Channel. Joan took up the battle alone, with the help of god and a few companions in arms. She convinced the bourgeoisie of Paris to open the gates of the city to the soldiers of the "only true king of France," and in 1429 she drove away the occupying army. In 1431, when Henry VI of England, who was then nine years old, was officially crowned king of France in Notre Dame, Joan of Arc was burned at the stake in Rouen. The courageous girl from Orléans was abandoned to her fate by everyone, including the man for whom she reconquered a city and a kingdom. Charles VII did not return to the capital until 1437, when he was sure that there was no longer any danger there. He was succeeded by Louis XI, a cruel and unscrupulous king, who entered Paris in 1461. The new monarch hated the city, a Paris reduced to a smelly, violent sewer in the hands of criminals of every stripe. For this reason, the king

installed the court in Bourges while the Louvre, degraded from the civil wars, became a sinister prison.

This was a turbulent time and the climate did not favor cultural life. Nonetheless a certain François Villon, a poet and con man who was fond of brawling and a was consummate scoundrel to boot, wrote the magnificent *Ballade des Pendus* in 1463 before being definitively thrown out of the city and disappearing without a trace. Meanwhile, in Mainz, Germany, Johannes Gutenberg invented a system of movable type characters that relegated monastic scribes to oblivion, creating in 1457 his first work, a 42-line Bible. The invention, which influenced the intellectual and literary life of Paris, was tried out in 1470 on the presses of the Sorbonne, where the first book published in France, the *Lettres Latines* by Bergame, was printed, and was almost immediately followed by a French translation of the Bible. Finally the common people could read sacred texts—on the condition that they knew how to read, a situation far from the reality of the age. Ninety-five percent of Parisians were completely illiterate at that time, while the numerous immigrants from distant regions like Pays d'Oc and Normandy had their own dialects. However, with the arrival of print shops and the growth of publishing houses, Paris became the center of European humanism. Pico della Mirandola, Erasmus, Ignatius of Loyola, Giordano Bruno, and many other contemporary philosophers visited there. Later, even Ronsard and Joachim du Bellay came there to write and to supervise their works in Paris.

33 **LEFT** FRANCIS I (1494–1547) WAS A GOOD KING AND A GREAT PATRON OF THE ARTS WHO ATTRACTED THE MOST FAMOUS EUROPEAN ARTISTS TO PARIS. IN 1540, HE RECEIVED EMPEROR CHARLES V, WHOSE TROOPS CROSSED HIS KINGDOM ON THEIR WAY TO PUNISH THE INHABITANTS OF GAND.

33 **RIGHT** PARIS IN 1500, AT THE BEGINNING OF THE REIGN OF LOUIS XII. THE LOUVRE, RUINED BY THE HUNDRED YEARS' WAR, HAD BECOME A MUNITIONS STOREHOUSE AND A DISTRICT PENITENTIARY. FRANCIS I HAD IT RESTORED.

THE RENAISSANCE OF FRANCIS I

In 1528, Francis I completed the capital and had the Louvre modified and then later reconstructed. This was the era of the high Renaissance, and the new city planning, inspired by the Italian model, was all the rage, while the architecture tended to full-blown Gothic. Old private palaces, ruined by wars and repeated plundering, were demolished, and new ones were built, including the beautiful Carnavalet mansion. Meanwhile, houses were perfectly aligned and their façades were rebuilt in brick. Paris, finally, had become Paris again, capital of the arts, letters, and elegance. Francis I created the Collège de France, oriented to a modern way of teaching, and he had French adopted as the official language in place of Latin. But war broke out again, this time against Italy and Spain, and the city had to be defended with new walls, reinforced with stone bastions in step with the progress of weaponry.

In 1549, Paris had about three hundred thousand inhabitants and ten thousand private dwellings of at least three stories, sixteen fountains, forty public baths, an aqueduct under construction, and about fifty religious buildings. In the same year, on the occasion of the triumphal entry of the new king, Henry II, the Fontaine des Innocents, a fountain near the wall encircling the Cimetière des Innocents, was inaugurated. The king attempted to improve the safety of the citizens by having lanterns lit by candles hung on the façades of houses and at street corners. He also created the *barrieres de sergents*, ancestors of the current police stations. He ordered the construction of the new City Hall, an official building worthy of what the good king called the "greatness of the capital," before his death in the Tournelles Palace from a trivial wound suffered in a tournament. His wife, Catherine de' Medici, had the building torn down, and established the Tuileries in its place.

Finally, as the last trace of the Renaissance in the city, the triumphal arch of Porte Saint-Antoine was built, which would serve as the model for those of Saint Denis and Saint Martin, built under Louis XIV.

Tolerant and open to new currents of thought, Paris

34 TOP In 1590, the League, a confederation created by Henry of Guise, marched through Paris to defend Catholicism against the Protestants and also to attempt to overthrow Henry IV in favor of the Duke of Guise. The League disappeared with the advent of Henry IV.

34 BOTTOM Catherine de' Medici instigated the Saint Bartholomew's Day Massacre, in which many Huguenots were killed.

welcomed the Reformation, but the antidogmatic ideas and the austerity it brought were displeasing to the populace, connected as it was to the external convenience of Catholic processions. It also frightened the nobility, uneasy with the power acquired by the new political-religious social order. A refutation surfaced as early as 1521, when the Sorbonne officially condemned the theses of Luther and, two years later, a Lutheran was put to death in the Place de Grève. The situation dragged on until 1572, when it degenerated into the Saint Bartholomew's Day Massacre, entirely organized and manipulated by Catherine de' Medici, mother of the successor to Henry II, Charles IX. The Protestants were hunted down in the streets of Paris, beaten to death, lynched, and butchered.

The slaughter lasted for five days and left four thousand dead, leading to the Wars of Religion.

Henry III, successor to Charles IX, was assassinated at Saint Cloud, and Henry of Navarre (Henry IV), a Protestant, succeeded him. Paris, however, rejected the Huguenot, preventing him from entering the city, so that he had to lay siege to Paris. For five months, the Parisians lived as they could, feeding themselves with dogs, cats, rats, roots, and even, it is said, a bread made with flour from the ossuary of the Cimetière des Innocents. The siege took nearly thirty thousand victims before Henry IV, moved by such tenacity, decided that "Paris is well worth a Mass" and converted to Catholicism. He entered the city on March 22, 1594, having himself proclaimed king in Notre Dame.

34-35   On March 22, 1594, after converting to Catholicism, Henry IV entered Paris. Henry IV was one of those monarchs who deeply loved Paris.

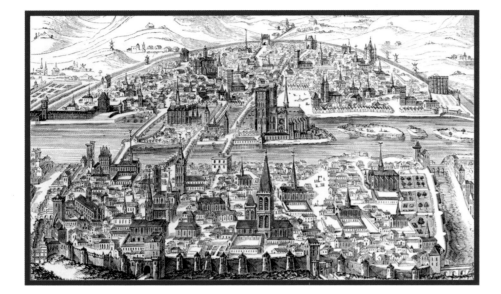

36 BOTTOM On May 14, 1610, the good king Henry IV was assassinated by Ravaillac right in the heart of Paris. Ravaillac was arrested, tortured, and then drawn and quartered publicly in the Place de Grève.

36-37 Paris in 1615 at the beginning of the reign of Louis XIII.

PARIS: WELL WORTH A MASS

Paris had, at that time, nearly 150,000 inhabitants. Henry IV fought poverty, creating a "placement office" where the unemployed of every sort and nationality could ask for work. Then he began to free the city from the ashes of war. He finished the Pont Neuf, replacing the houses with broad sidewalks, and he completed the work on City Hall. He connected the two small islands of the Île de la Cité, creating Place Dauphine, and he joined the Île aux-Vaches and the Île Notre-Dame to make the Île Saint-Louis, which he covered with magnificent homes. He had the Place Royale (now Place des Vosges) designed and laid the basis for the elegant quarter of Marais, where nobles, magistrates,

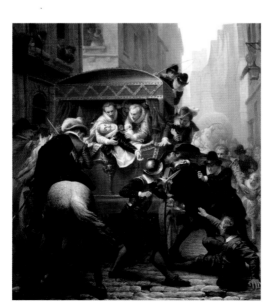

financiers, and important government officials built their homes. He created the Hôpital Saint-Louis and insisted that, for hygienic reasons, isolated rooms be reserved for contagious patients. He created the great arteries—a hundred of them in only fifty years—and brought fresh air into the streets by demolishing illegal buildings so that traffic circulated more freely. In an irony of sorts, in 1610, a bottleneck in traffic that blocked the royal carriage in the middle of the Halles quarter allowed Henry IV to be attacked and killed by François Ravaillac. The Coeur Couronné, the hotel to which he was taken, still exists; on the pavement is a star reminding Parisians of the tragic end of a king who truly loved his capital.

LE PLAN DE LA VILLE CITE VNIVERSITE ET FAVXBOVRGS DE PARIS AVEC LA DESCRIPTION DE SON ANTIQVITE
ET SINGVLLARITES

RICHELIEU'S CITY

Louis XIII, aided by Richelieu, completed Henry IV's work. The city then extended in all directions, and the suburbs of Montmartre and Saint Honoré were created. Work began on the construction of Pont Marie, which was inaugurated in 1635, and an equestrian statue of Henry IV was placed at the entrance to Pont Neuf. Religious architecture was also thriving. Between 1600 and 1639, sixty convents opened, including that of the Ursulines. Paris became a holy city under the influence of Anne of Austria, the queen, a fervently religious woman who, at the birth of her first son, the future King Louis XIV, gave thanks to god by having Val de Grâce built. Churches were consecrated nonstop, and miraculous cures, real or presumed, had people talking. Witches and fortune-tellers were burned in Place de Grève or at the Contrescarpe while religious orders multiplied. The Jesuits gravitated around the centers of power and fought theological battles against the Jansenists, a religious movement introduced by Mother Angelica Arnauld in 1540. Saint Vincent de Paul—foreshadowing Abbé Pierre—was a national hero. He created medical and charitable foundations, such as Enfants Trouvés, nicknamed les Poulbots, the Parisian "guttersnipes."

In 1622, Paris, the religious city, became an archbishopric. In 1631, Paris, the intellectual city, gave permission to Théophraste Renaudot to publish the *Gazette de France*, the first weekly publication sold in the city and the only one authorized by the king. Unfortunately, the people were poor and illiterate. Despite the existence of free religious schools, illiteracy was an endemic evil. The city had four hundred thousand inhabitants, most of whom had not received any benefit from the wealth generated by the social and political changes. France was at war with England and Spain, and refugees were arriving en masse, recounting the horrors perpetrated in the provinces. The Parisians, taken by surprise, raised barricades in case the enemy presented itself at the city gates. Meanwhile the intellectual elite struggled under the dome of the French Academy for the "true definition of linguistic words," while the nobility amused itself in fencing competitions using foils with buttons since dueling had been prohibited some years before. In the poorer quarters, people died of hunger or violence. At the Jeu de Paume, the bourgeoisie and the nobility paid honors to *Le Cid*, a work by Pierre Corneille. Its first presentation was followed by a refined dinner for five hundred people, presided over by the king.

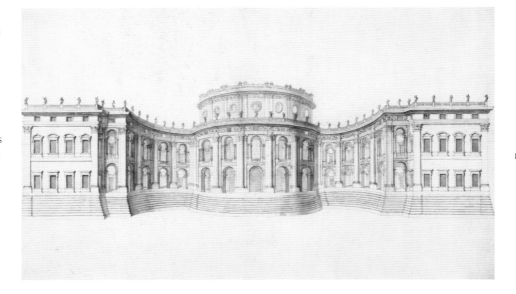

THE SUN KING

Richelieu died in December 1642 and Louis XIII in May 1643. Louis XIV succeeded to the throne though he was only five years old. It was his mother, Anne of Austria, who ensured the regency, conferring the power on Cardinal Mazarin. The court left the Louvre to move to the modern Palais Royale. Nonetheless Mazarin's reign began badly. At first the Parisians, who detested him, limited themselves to mocking the prelate with clandestine libels. Then they protested. "Too many taxes, too many wars, too much poverty," chanted thousands of protesters under Anne of Austria's windows. Instigated by members of Parliament, princes, and dissident nobles, the populace revolted. This was the Fronde, which brought on an economic crisis and aggravated the poverty of the people. The city finally submitted itself to the king, who had taken refuge at Saint Germain en Laye, and Louis XIV returned to the capital on July 2, 1652, acclaimed by the crowd. The sovereign installed himself at the Louvre, which, though sad and cold, was safer than the Palais Royale. He named Jean-Baptiste Colbert "regulator of construction, arts, tapestries, and manu-

facturing in France." Together they decided to beautify the city, and Paris once again became an enormous construction site. A city plan was adopted that provided for the creation of a perimeter delimited by boulevards beyond which construction was not allowed. Within that perimeter, Louis XIV ordered large works, including the creation of Place Vendôme, Place des Victoires, and Place des Invalides and the restoration of the Louvre. The latter, however, was abandoned, leaving the north wing uncovered when the king went to Versailles. Jules Hardouin-Mansart rebuilt the suburbs of Saint Germain and Saint Honoré, connecting them by the Pont Royal and giving his name to mansards, the garrets that follow the slope of the roof. Andre Le Nôtre created parks and gardens, among them the Jardin des Plantes, knocking down working-class houses whose occupants, however, he forgot to relocate. Artisan quarters were created and privileges bestowed upon the inhabitants. Cabinetmakers and manufacturers of glass and mirrors installed themselves in Faubourg Saint-Antoine, where they are still found today.

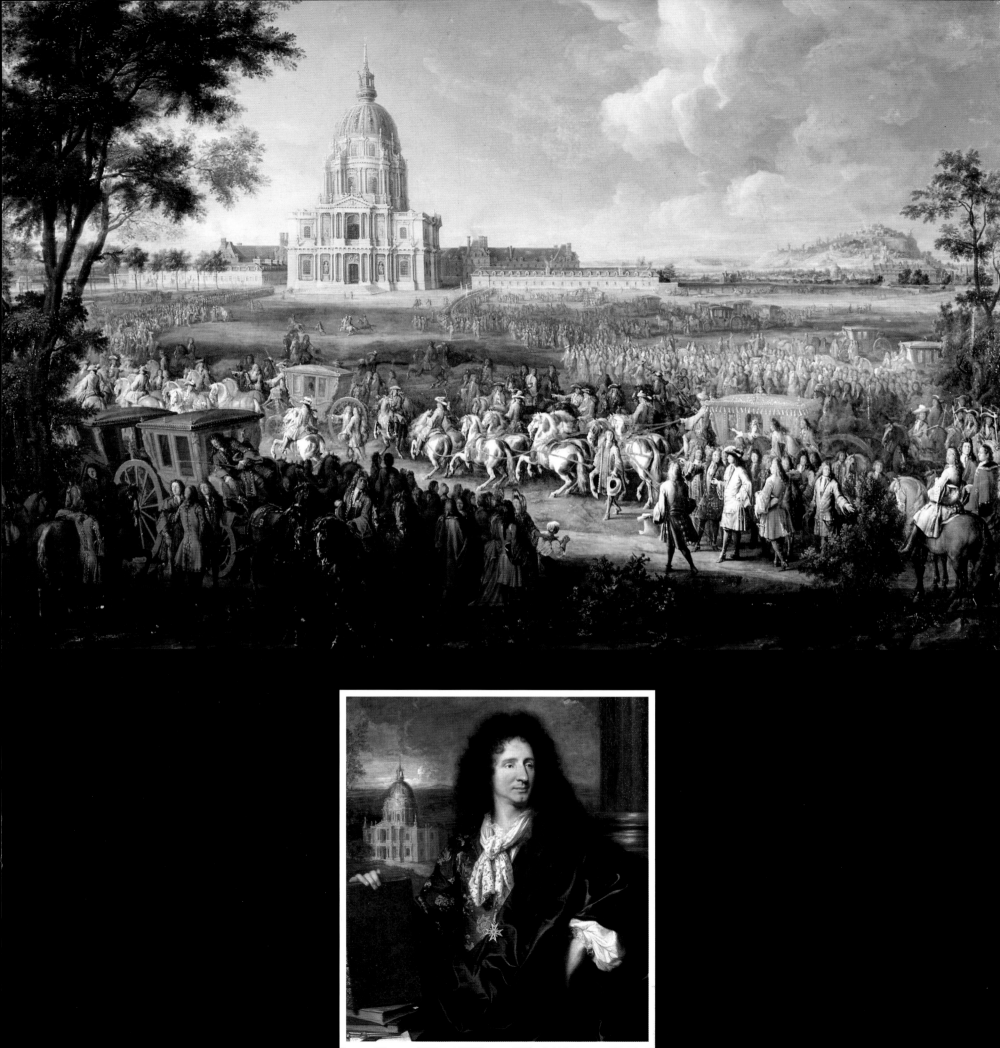

42-43 In 1672, Louis XIV inaugurated the Observatory constructed by Claude Perrault. No iron whatsoever was used in building it, so as not to disrupt the magnetized needles of the instruments used for astronomical observations.

43 LEFT Louis XIV prided himself on being a great patron of the sciences, arts, and culture. In the company of his favorite, Mme. de Maintenon, he listened to Racine declaim the now famous *Athalie* verses.

Louis XIV, who prided himself on being a patron of the arts, opened academies of music and dance, painting ateliers, and theatrical courses in quantity. Literary salons abounded, and there was no modest bourgeois who did not dream of having one of his or her own. In these salons, the reputations of the great minds of that time were made and unmade, in particular at the home of Catherine de Vivonne, at the Rambouillet Palace, at Madeleine de Scudéry's, and at the Marais Palace, where Racine and Molière were often guests.

The refinement of the capital was as extreme as was the indigence of the people. The army was no longer paid but only fed (and poorly so). The bourgeoisie was tiring of financially supporting Louis XIV's megalomaniac follies and the wastefulness of his courtiers. Life in Paris had become expensive, and there was a shortage of wheat and meat. The terrible floods of 1658 destroyed Pont Marie and swept away the quarters along the riverside, throwing thousands of desperate souls into streets that were already teeming with beggars.

But the Parisians, who were easily satisfied, became ecstatic about the royal fireworks (put on just for their benefit). They also discovered coffee, served in bars that became fashionable meeting places. In 1675, you could count two hundred coffee houses, including the famous Procope, the haunt of the intellectual elite. In private mansions, receptions were sumptuous. Louis XIV loved magnificence as much as his frivolous court, which became passionate about joking, royal tennis, and *boules.*

The king put an end to the war with Spain by marrying Maria Teresa d'Austria, but the marriage was celebrated at Saint Jean de Luz in the Low Countries, something that accentuated the grumbling of the populace.

Then, finally, a semblance of peace returned.

43 RIGHT Louis XIV liked Molière, who made him "laugh so much." Still, Molière, who died on the stage in 1673, was exposed to the attacks of detractors all his life. His body, like those of all theatrical people of that time, was thrown into a common grave.

44 TOP RIGHT On September 2, 1667, the police lieutenant Nicola de la Reynie lit one of the 2,136 lanterns that would light the 912 streets of Paris.

44 BOTTOM At the foot of the Hôtel de Ville, in what was known as Place de Grève in the seventeenth century and was used for executions, commoners enjoyed a public holiday.

45 TOP The Louvre, about 1665, seen from the Pont Neuf. Great liveliness ruled on the bridge where the equestrian statue of Henry IV dominated the scene. Cast by Jean Boulogne in 1614, it was the first public statue in Paris.

45 BOTTOM In this view of rue Saint Antoine as it appeared in the seventeenth century, an anonymous painter has portrayed the jests and games of a lively "court of miracles" of commoners. At the time, Paris had a population of 450,000.

Paris was by then a sprawling city and it was growing inordinately in population, in no small part due to the immigration of people from the provinces who, attracted by the glitter of the capital, tried to survive as best they could. In 1671, the year in which Louis XIV sumptuously installed himself in Versailles, Paris had 450,000 inhabitants, divided among 45,000 dwellings. This meant that the common people slept under bridges more often than in good beds. As for the city police, there were only four hundred archers on foot, flanked by a brigade of cavalry for the night rounds. In short, the working-class neighborhoods were places of ill repute where pickpockets laid down the law and where the provosts were not always able to disperse the myriad "miracle courts," motley crowds of beggars and brigands that formed spontaneously. In the course of a single year, 1669, the Grand Provost had 4,800 vagabonds and prostitutes locked up in the Hôpital Général, but since there were no guards, the prisoners quickly found themselves back on the streets. Nonetheless, some measures were adopted to protect the safety of the Parisians. The Grand Provost authorized the creation of a corps of torchbearers who accompanied people home at night for a few coins. Meanwhile, the king had ordered the placement of metallic lanterns at street corners to illumi-

nate Parisian nights. In 1662, there were nearly three thousand of them. In the same year, the first *carrosses a cinq sols* (five-penny carriages) appeared, inexpensive vehicles that followed pre-established routes, anticipating our modern means of public transportation.

The end of the reign of Louis XIV was marked by a return to austerity, even to excessive religiosity, under the moralistic influence of Madame de Maintenon, who had secretly married the king in 1683. When she was still merely one of the king's favorites, Madame had condemned literary salons, and literary salons disappeared. But what was worse, in 1685, she convinced the king to revoke the Edict of Nantes signed by Henry IV, thus forcing sixteen thousand of the thirty thousand Protestants in Paris to emigrate to Germany, Holland, and Switzerland, where they stirred up great hostility to the French monarchy. This error, one of the most serious in the politics of Louis XIV, would have tragic social and economic consequences. It was the twilight for the Sun King, who had lost his splendor. If people were still dancing at Versailles, the violins were playing melancholy music. Paris, abandoned to her fate, was vulnerable and exposed to any catastrophe. The most frightening was the terrible winter of 1709 when, between January and March, more than thirty thousand people died of cold and hunger.

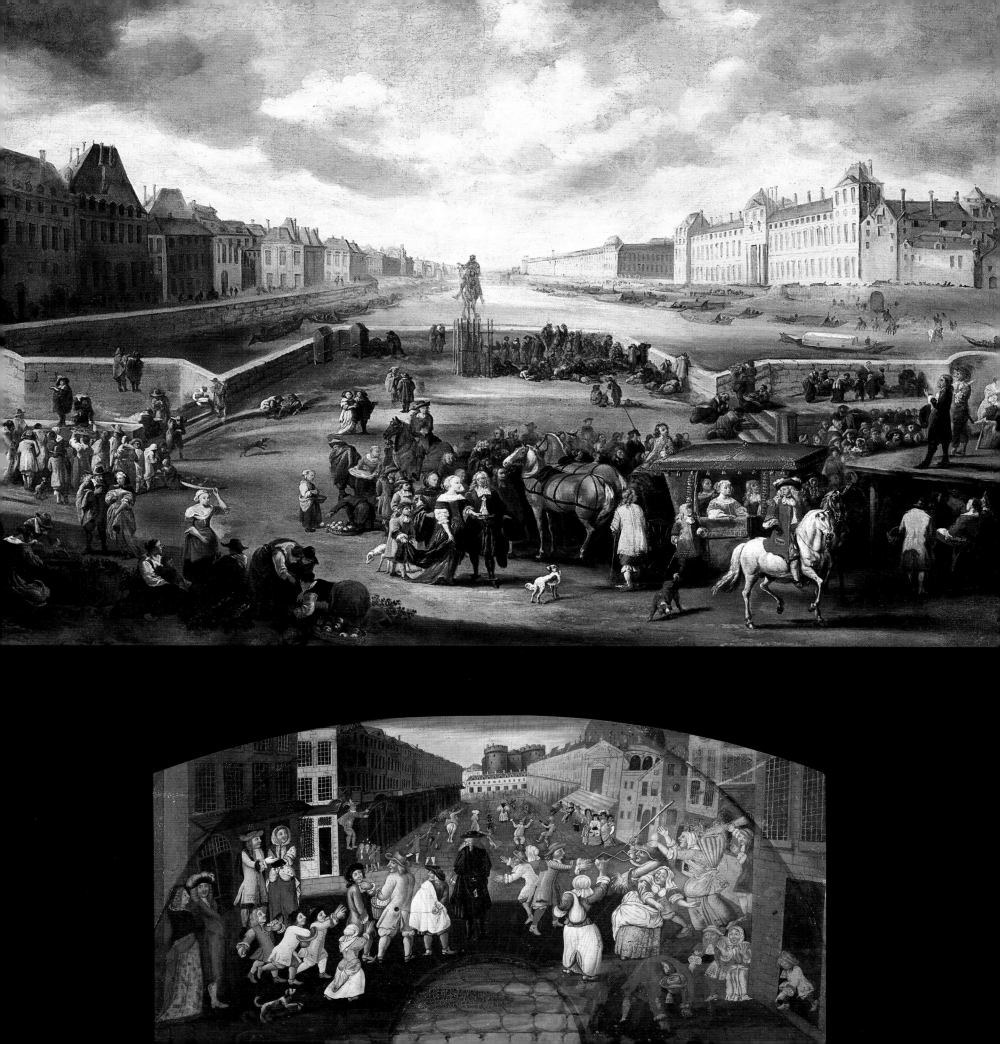

THE CENTURY OF LIGHTS

Louis XIV died in 1715 and was succeeded by his great-grandson, Louis XV, the Well-Beloved, the king who was to make Paris the "Ville Lumière," the City of the Enlightenment. The new age had begun with Philip d'Orléans, the debauched, dissolute regent who liberalized customs, reopening the literary and fashionable salons and calling back to Paris artists and creators who had vanished. The removal of the court to Versailles had not deprived the city of its intellectual and artistic supremacy. On the contrary, it gave Paris a rebellious and irreverent Frondeur mentality, which led to accepting new ideas naturally.

The reign of Louis XV began with his installation at the Tuileries. But soon he, too, went to Versailles. The populace mocked everything and everyone, and once again abandoned to its fate, Paris let itself be influenced by the Encyclopedists, the philosophers who freely expressed themselves in the great literary salons of the opulent bourgeoisie, fostering the circulation of the political ideas that led to the Revolution.

But all that was not enough to make the people happier. Hunger and poverty were still the fate of those with no property, the poor, who, being unable to feed their babies, abandoned them at convent doors. In one year alone, 1720, the number of foundlings amounted to six thousand. The struggle against poverty was, as usual, fought through charity and repression. An edict obliged those with an income to give one-thirtieth of it to help the parishes succor the poor. Cohorts of prostitutes and beggars were deported to Canada and Louisiana. In 1778, the Mont de Piété, a royal pawnshop, was inaugurated to help the needy.

The processions were innumerable. The relics of Sainte Geneviève were carried through the streets of the capital, in a collective climate of hysteria and religious fanaticism. Unfortunately, however, where men are impotent even the patron saint will fail.

The populace then decided to amuse itself, dancing quadrilles to the sound of Italian accordions, attending the theaters, of which there were about ten, and listening to free concerts in the public gardens. They went mad for everything that took them away from their daily troubles: the flight of Pilâtre de Rozier from the Champ-de-Mars aboard a hot air balloon; the arrest of Cartouche, a good-hearted bandit loved by the crowd; and the great public executions, such as that of Damien, a presumed regicide, drawn and quartered in the Place de Grève in 1757. Not even these diversions, however, were enough. Day after day, gripped by hunger and crushed by poverty, the people of Paris began to rebel. These were brief insurrections but each one had its share of victims.

Let's return to 1728, the year in which Louis XV's interest in the city was aroused and the king had the first street signs hung. In 1748, the sovereign laid the cornerstone of the Church of Sainte Geneviève, which became the Panthéon during the Revolution. In 1758, he inaugurated work for the Place de la Concorde, followed by the Théâtre de l'Odéon, the École Militaire and the esplanade of Champ-de-Mars. The longer he reigned, the more the monarch listened to new ideas dealing with the relationship between the city and its citizens. Monuments were no longer built solely for aesthetic reasons, but also for their usefulness and social significance. At the death of Louis XV in 1774, modern city planning had been born. But at what price?

48 On July 14, 1789, the Parisians, in search of arms, took control of the Bastille after sacking the Tuileries.

49 LEFT Louis XVI (1754–1793). The Convention unanimously voted to execute him: he was guillotined in the Place de la Concorde on January 21, 1793. His execution led to the coalition of European sovereigns against the French revolutionaries.

49 RIGHT On December 2, 1804, Napoleon Bonaparte, from minor Corsican nobility, proclaimed himself emperor of the French and also crowned his wife Joséphine de Beauharnais before Pope Pius VII. For the occasion, Cherubini conducted the first performance of Mozart's *Requiem*.

THE DAYS OF THE "MARSEILLAISE"

When Louis XVI rose to power, he found the coffers empty and Paris, which then had nearly a million inhabitants, decidedly badly off. Certainly, the city was changing, but the suffering of the people was the same. The rental buildings erected in place of the old dwellings of the Palais Royale were not for them. Neither was white bread, the price of which had become exorbitant. Paris grumbled and then snarled. Everything was in place for the curtain to be raised on the Revolution.

It was 1789. Exasperated by famine and injustice, Paris arose in one of those insurrections of which it alone knows the secret. Receptive to the ideas circulating in the cafés, aroused by orators such as Desmoulins, Marat, Danton, Hébert, and Robespierre, the city took up arms, stormed the Bastille, proclaimed the first republican prefect, locked the king and his family in the Tuileries, and entered the convents, appropriating the goods of the clergy. It imposed the bases of the new order—freedom, equality, fraternity—that were inscribed on the façades of monuments while Rouget de l'Isle sang

the "Marseillaise" in a parlor in Faubourg Poissonniere. The Revolution, however, slipped and lost its footing. The city was the site of internal party struggles—Jacobins and Cordeliers against the Girondists. Paris plunged into the Terror. The guillotine was everywhere: at the Carrousel, in Place de Grève, at the Concorde, and even in the engine room of the Louvre. On September 21, 1792, the Republic was proclaimed amidst general jubilee. The king, whose flight to Varennes had failed, was guillotined in the Place de la Concorde on January 21, 1793. By 1794, 1,306 prisoners had been executed, not all of them nobles or magistrates. When Napoleon Bonaparte made his appearance, Paris was prostrate, famished, ruined, wounded, and deluded by the revolutionary torment. All that time, the city had experienced the depths of misery and had no more than six hundred thousand inhabitants, one-fifth of whom were registered as destitute. The nobility, the clergy, and the large traditional bourgeoisie were absent from the new social fabric. Meanwhile the army controlled the city like a conqueror, carrying out looting and extortion of every type. On a cultural level, the Revolution had changed nothing. Two out of five Parisians were illiterate, and only twenty free schools existed. Despite everything, with that sense of humor and sense of life that characterize them, the Parisians tried to forget their hunger and poverty by enjoying themselves. They improvised balls at the Palais Royale or in parks or gardens where they could make fun of the Incroyables and the Merveilleuses, eccentric young people who affected extravagance in their way of dressing. Twelve municipalities were created, which later would be transformed into *arrondissements* (administrative areas). Bonaparte's coup d'état succeeded among the general indifference. He took power and the reins of the city in 1799. In 1804 he proclaimed himself Emperor Napoleon I and crowned himself in Notre Dame.

THE CAPITAL OF THE EMPIRE

Wars resumed: Napoleon sacked Europe, bringing back treasures that he exhibited at the Louvre so that the Parisians could admire them. During his reign, city planning developed in grand style, even though economic recessions and costly military campaigns often interrupted ambitious projects like the Stock Exchange, the Arc de Triomphe, the Place de l'Étoile, and the Madeleine. These plans would be finished under later reigns.

Napoleon dedicated monuments of his victories to the city: the Vendôme Column, the bridges of Saint Louis, Austerlitz, and Iéna, as well as the rue de Rivoli. The first covered walkways, du Caire and des Panoramas, also appeared, as well as a numbering system for houses. In 1813, Bonaparte could not stop an invasion of France. The following year, the Cossacks camped on the Champs Elysées and left Paris one of its most popular words—*bistro*.

Napoleon died in Saint Helena in 1821, but it was not until 1840 that his ashes returned to Paris, to the Invalides. When the monarchy was restored in 1814, one of Louis XVIII's first gestures was to build a monument to Louis XVI. Then, the new sovereign committed himself to bringing order to the city. But neither he nor Charles X, who succeeded him, was concerned about changing its appearance or controlling its urban design. Private construction grew quickly, fed by the creation of the first banks. Paris fitted itself out with buildings of a pleasing style and small shops on the outskirts surrounded by little gardens in the quarters of Beaujon, de l'Europe, and Saint Georges.

Two societies confronted each other: the refined traditional bourgeoisie, tied to their privileges and returned to the fold with the restoration of the monarchy, together with the *nouveaux riche*, the new, greedy bourgeoisie described so well by Emile Zola, which would come to victory under Louis Philippe, versus the array of modest functionaries and the miserable proletariat who crammed the quarters in the city center, and who were often the subject of stories by Eugène Sue and Victor Hugo. Saint Meri and the Île de la Cité were then lairs in which alcoholism, prostitution, and crime were rife, and whose residents were devastated by tuberculosis and syphilis. In 1832, a cholera epidemic took 44,000 victims, eighty percent of whom were buried in common graves. The desperate once again rebelled and took to the streets, clubs in hand, to reclaim their rights. In 1830, the revolution called the Trois Glorieuses (three glorious days, July 27–29) broke out. The names of its victims are engraved on a commemorative column on the Place de la Bastille.

It was necessary to wait for Napoleon III, who came to power in 1852 and intiated the large construction works of the second Republic, for Paris to change its appearance significantly. With disconcerting rapidity, Alphand, Belgrand, and Haussmann remodeled the city, making it a modern capital. They knocked down the unhealthy quarters and opened the broad boulevards of Sébastopol, Saint Michel, Magenta, and Saint Germain and restructured rue de Rivoli. Meanwhile the public streets were paved and graced with tree-lined sidewalks. The city was practically razed to the ground and then rebuilt. Lovely freestone buildings with sculpted façades arose everywhere. Baltard designed the new East and North stations and the large *halles* of the main market, metal pavilions that are incredibly light and bright.

Large department stores opened: le Bon Marché, les Trois Quartiers, le Printemps, la Samaritaine. Garnier began constructing the Opéra. Violet Ledue finished the restoration of Notre Dame. Paris was lit by lamps, first powered by gas and then, in 1878, by electricity. The Place de l'Opéra was the first to try out the "magic light" amid the exclamations of amazement from a dazzled population. The lungs of the city were the Bois de Vincennes, the Bois de

Boulogne, the Buttes-Chaumont, Parc Monceau, and Parc Montsouris. Father Lachaise allowed the old small cemeteries to be reclaimed. In 1867, the first *bateaux-mouches*, the characteristic boats for river cruises, sailed on the Seine. In 1869, Paris boasted a world record: 373 miles of underground sewers in a city that was an immense construction site in which everything was open to experiment. Paris was an intellectual and artistic center unparalleled in Europe, with figures like Théodore Géricault, Alphonse Lamartine, Victor Hugo, Charles Baudelaire, Paul Verlaine, and Louis Daguerre, who took the first photograph ever made on the boulevard du Temple. It was also the site of the grandiose Universal Expositions, visited even by reigning European royalty. The Champs Elysées was *the* fashionable street, the place to see and be seen.

According to an estimate, the Parisians in 1846 numbered nearly two million. In less than fifty years, the population had doubled. Life was expensive. Supporting yourself was not easy, and the conditions in which those excluded from the great innovative works lived were terrible: 258,000 families without resources, which explains why, in one year alone—1847—a million and a half objects were pawned at Mont de Piété.

THE UNIVERSAL EXPOSITION

In 1870, Prussia defeated France. Napoleon III fell, and the government of Adolphe Thiers negotiated with the enemy to encircle and bomb Paris. The city resisted at first. But the winter was hard, and soon the Parisians were reduced to hunger. The exotic animals from the Jardin des Plantes were sold for their weight in gold while cats, dogs, rats, and birds were the daily bread of the most fortunate. On March 1, the city capitulated. Prussians marched along the Champs Elysées. The nearly moribund city suffered from terrible privation until, in 1871, laborers, artisans, and small businessmen, in a desperate attempt to influence the course of history as the sansculottes had during the Revolution, rebelled: this was the Commune. Federates and Communards burned City Hall and the Tuileries, setting off an urban guerilla war against the regular army sent from Versailles, to which Thiers had retreated. Marshall MacMahon, aided by the Prussians, brutally put down the insurrection: forty thousand victims killed in one week and five thousand Communards deported to the colonies or to the Cayenne penal settlement. Half of the experienced laborers fled the city to find their fortunes in the southern provinces.

Dominated, Paris remained in a state of siege until the election of president Jules Grévy in 1876.

"People of Paris, you sleep with only one eye closed," wrote Zola. How true! In 1890, laborers, up in arms because of the new socialist ideas, took to the streets to demand—and obtain—an eight-hour working day.

Time went on, and Paris soon forgot about the insurrections. The new century was approaching. In 1889, Sadi Carnot became president, inaugurating the Universal Exposition that led to erecting the most famous monument in the city—the tower built by Gustave Eiffel to celebrate the hundredth anniversary of the Revolution.

The 1900 International Exposition gave the city the Grand and Petit Palais, the Alexander III bridge, and the Métro, the metropolitan underground railway.

FIGARO ILLUSTRÉ

At the beginning of the twentieth century, Paris was the center of cosmopolitan culture where the entire world paraded. The Belle Époque had arrived. The city was the international capital of the arts and fashion. Painters, writers, architects, poets, and philosophers met at Montmartre and at Montparnasse. They included Braque, Vlaminck, Kupka, and Juan Gris. The impressionists, the fauves, and the abstract painters had important social positions. Henri de Toulouse-Lautrec was inspired by the dancers of the Moulin Rouge. Pablo Picasso painted *Les Demoiselles d'Avignon*, which marked the beginning of Cubism. Mucha designed the first advertising posters for Sarah Bernhardt at the height of her glory. Literature was at its peak, introducing authors like Guillaume Apollinaire, Max Jacob, Mac Orlan, and others. Hector Guimard experimented with the *nouille* style of Art Nouveau, creating elaborate buildings, among them the famous Castel Béranger on rue Lafontaine—at the time made people laugh, but now it is rightfully protected. Auguste Perret built the admirable Champs Elysée theater. Meanwhile, the cinema, the first performance of which was held at the Grand Café in 1895, attracted crowds. The first movie theater was opened by the Lumière brothers on boulevard Saint Denis. Then Léon Gaumont set up studios at Buttes-Chaumont and, in 1911, in Place Clichy, to inaugurate the progenitor of cinematic complexes, the Gaumont Palace, with 3,400 seats.

The first telegraphic connection between the Eiffel Tower and the Panthéon dates to 1898. It saved the tower, which proved to be an exceptional antenna, from demolition! In the same year, Louis Renault built a car at Billancourt. In 1914, his factory employed four thousand people, completely occupying the Ilot Seguin. In 1895, at the Tuileries, the first Motor Show was so crowded that a hundred people were injured.

An insatiable giant, Paris always welcomed. Initially there were the Alvernians, immediately nicknamed *bougnats*, and the coal merchants, who specialized in the sale of wood to burn and in running the *bistros*, the taverns. Then came the Bretons, followed by the Belgians, Italians, and Germans. It was an exciting period but one that was also marked by large migrations toward the *zones*, suburbs that were growing up on outskirts farthest from the capital: Saint Ouen, la Villette, Montreuil. It was the era of the *fortifs*, the fortifications, where *argot*, a popular dialect invented by rude youngsters and bad boys was spoken and where the bourgeoisie went to flood the ballroom of Lape or to the Echaudettes.

CINÉMATOGRAPHE LUMIÈRE

60 BOTTOM August 1914: war is declared and Gallieni turns Paris into an entrenched camp. Trenches are dug just outside the city and the main monuments —the Arc de Triomphe du Carrousel is shown here—are protected.

61 TOP November 11, 1918: armistice is declared and the streets of Paris are wild with excitement. The population cheers the Allies and waves French, English, and American flags.

61 BOTTOM At the end of 1920, an urn containing the heart of Léon Gambetta, who had died in 1882, was moved to the Pantheon. Fifty years before, the politician had proclaimed the Third Republic, marking the end of the empire founded by Bonaparte.

60 TOP LEFT Paris prepares for war: Gallieni had staples of all kinds brought to the capital: flour, firewood, and even wine, whose barrels blocked the Bercy riverfront.

60 TOP RIGHT July 14, 1919: Clemenceau has a pile of artillery pieces, taken from the Germans, placed on the circle of the Champs Elysées. Several spectators clamber to the top to watch the triumphant parade of the Allied troops.

THE END OF THE BELLE ÉPOQUE

The First World War brutally interrupted the Belle Époque. The German Big Bertha bombed Paris, and the skies filled with zeppelins. Private taxis took soldiers to the front at Marnes and women took the jobs of the men who had left for the war, driving trams or working as laborers at Renault or Citroën.

The capital became an important economic center, almost exclusively for the wartime industry. Paris was hungry; Paris was cold. As though the burden of suffering that accompanies all wars was not enough, a viral flu called the Spanish flu hit the city, causing more than two thousand deaths in a few days.

Shaky, subjected to rationing, and hungry, despite everything Paris welcomed the exodus. First the Belgians, attempting to escape from the invasion of their country, then the Poles, the Rumanians, the Hungarians, the Russians escaping from the October 1917 revolution, and finally those from the provinces of Artois, Flanders, Champagne, and Marne. The city became over-populated, the poverty was dire, people managed the best they could. Exasperated by all sorts of hardships, the populace grumbled, then roared: sporadic revolts broke out that came to nothing.

The sun did not shine on the gray city until the armistice in 1919. An enormous procession reunited the Parisians on the Champs Elysées. In 1920, under the Arc de Triomphe, the body of an unknown soldier was buried in memory of those killed in the conflict. It seems that it might have been a German soldier.

63 TOP LEFT French singer and dancer Mistinguett, née Jeanne-Marie Bourgeois (1874–1956), was one of the top stars of variety shows in the Twenties and Thirties.

Paris came out of the Great War with an insatiable hunger for life. The Années Folles had begun. Women emancipated themselves, cut their hair in a "little-boy" style, and shortened their skirts. The queens of France were Coco Chanel, the designer, and the performers Edith Piaf and Mistinguett. Chez Maxim hosted divas and royalty and, while the champagne flowed like a river among the rich, torrents of red wine warmed the hearts of the poor.

Elections followed one after the other and demonstrations did, too. Often they ended badly. In 1936, the Popular Front called for strikes and occupation of factories, demanding paid holidays. It got them. That summer Parisians sang along with Charles Trenet and Maurice Chevalier, happily pedaling along the roads of France.

The 1937 Exhibition, in which Stalin's USSR and Hitler's Nazi Germany participated, turned out to be a fiasco and a wreck for the finances of Paris. But it left the city the palaces of Chaillot and Tokyo in addition to a vague memory of having seen *Guernica*, Picasso's famous painting, for the first time.

63 TOP CENTER American singer and dancer Josephine Baker (1906–1975) first went onstage at the Folies Bergère in the mid-Twenties, and quickly became the darling of Parisian audiences.

63 TOP RIGHT The unmistakable style created by Coco Chanel, the unforgettable "Mademoiselle" of French haute couture, is trendy even today. Her pet phrase was "Fashion passes, but style remains."

63 BOTTOM Mistinguett—actress, singer, dancer, and star of Paris revues at the turn of the century—is captured here in an unusual pose, in a scene from a film by Georges Méliès, a precursor of science-fiction movies.

64 TOP June 13, 1940: Paris is an open city. German troops goose-step down the Champs Elysées. Two days later, the Armistice is signed at Rethondes.

64 BOTTOM June 23, 1940: Hitler visits Paris, Les Invalides, Napoleon's Tomb, the Eiffel Tower, and the Trocadero. Vichy is the new capital of France, governed by Marshal Pétain.

65 TOP LEFT August 25, 1944: Paris revolts and fighting breaks out across the city. The rebels bring out their weapons and wait for the armor-plated vehicles of General Leclerc. General von Choltitz signs the surrender for Germany.

In 1938, Paris had more than three million inhabitants. Parisians danced the Charleston, but on the edge of a volcano that exploded in 1939. The city sank into that *drôle de guerre.* Strange, the war.

Occupied by the Germans in 1940, the capital went through the usual sequence of deprivation, bombardment, and humiliation. It lived through the shame of the Hebrew Statute and the dishonor of the police who participated in the Vélodrome d'Hiver roundup. The Resistance became organized, despite arrests, torture, and summary executions. Paris was torn apart, mocked and gagged, murmuring the "Marseilles" and partisans' songs through clenched teeth whenever Gestapo officials passed by. Paris, courageous, with thousands of anonymous actions that saved Jews from the convoys for Auschwitz. Paris, coquettish, with young women who painted the lines of imaginary hosiery on their leg, with creators of fashion Jacques Fath and Christian Dior, with inventors of artificial yarn made from raw vegetable material. Paris, rebellious, secretly publishing Sartre and Camus.

Thanks to the German military governor von Choltiz, the capital was not burned. General Leclerc entered the city on August 24, 1944. A free Paris jubilantly welcomed American soldiers and General de Gaulle, who the next day triumphantly walked down the Champs Elysées and was acclaimed by more than a million and a half people.

65 TOP RIGHT August 29, 1944: Paris is liberated. A German air strike kills 200 people. Several German soldiers try to block a procession of Parisians on their way to the Hôtel de Ville, but are killed by the enraged crowd.

65 BOTTOM The liberated Parisians overrun the Champs Elysées and welcome the triumphant General De Gaulle, who walks from Notre Dame to the Arc de Triomphe. However, the Germans continue to bomb the capital, killing 189 people.

As always, Paris pulled itself together. At Saint Germain des Près, in the jazz circles Tabou and Rose Rouge, in the fashionable cafés Deux Magots and Flore, it invented a new way of living. Existentialism had its popes: Greco, Vian, Jean-Paul Sartre, Simone de Beauvoir. Paris was a great festival. But the circulation of live shows changed with the arrival of television in 1949, when the first newscast was transmitted.

After the war came the reconstruction; Paris was lagging behind most European cities. It began by knocking down a hundred thousand unhealthy habitations and hiring young architects to design a modern city that, though remaining the capital of France, would come out of its isolation and open itself to the outside. It improved its means of communication. In record time, a ring road was built and so were highways and airports. Towers and new buildings sprang up like mushrooms. Montparnasse; the Front de Seine; the quarters of Flandres, Italie, de la Défense; the Palais des Congrès at Porte Maillot; and the Maison de la Radio, immediately nicknamed "the Camembert," all appeared. In 1969, work began on the Centre Beaubourg, built in the area of the Marché des Halles, which had moved to Rungis.

Paris prided itself on gigantism, especially under the presidency of Georges Pompidou, who left the city a *bétonné* ("exemplary" but also "cemented") style, contested especially because it made the city lose much of its soul. Paris was rehabilitated and renewed, often without consulting the Parisians. These were the same determined Parisians who, for months, mobilized themselves, blocking rue d'Alésia and preventing the bulldozers from destroying the charming Cité des Plantes. Rental prices forced the classes with a moderate income to emigrate toward the outskirts, where they built immense and mediocre housing complexes, dormitory towns that became the focus of opposition and violence.

Between 1945 and 1968, the capital exasperatedly lived through the ups and downs of both internal and international politics. Since 1950, Algeria had been at the center of concerns. Paris saw her sons leave for the far-off *gebel*, and many never returned. In the 1960s, sporadic anti-Algerian demonstrations broke out and were repressed—or, on occasion, organized by the powers-that-be. The city was no longer safe, and a curfew was announced. The OAS (the right-wing Secret Army Organization) terrorized the people with its bloody actions.

The Algerian war ended in 1969, and the exodus of the *pieds noirs*, the French Algerians fleeing from that land, assailed the Sentier quarter. Paris then experienced an extraordinary mixture of ethnic groups, destined over time to become accentuated. Today, only one in four Parisians is a native.

"When Paris sneezes, France blows its nose," claimed General de Gaulle. The capital did that in 1968 when the universities of Nanterre and the Sorbonne reached the boiling point. The Latin Quarter was covered with barricades in front of which students tangled with the police. All of France came to a halt. Planes did not fly, public transportation stopped, the trains were blocked, and the shops were closed. But the Parisians sang and danced in factory courtyards.

Paris exited unharmed from yet another conflict, which, as always, though leaving indelible traces, did not affect its thirst for life and the energy of its people.

68 RIGHT 1989: Paris lavishly celebrates the 200th anniversary of the French Revolution. The Arche de la Défense was inaugurated on July 13th, and its terrace offered the seventeen heads of state invited to the celebration a unique panoramic view of the capital.

68-69 Mayor Jacques Chirac presents a plastic model of the renovation of the quarter of Beaubourg, whose market Les Halles was torn down in 1969 and moved to Rungis.

In 1977, Paris became a commune with twenty-one municipalities, and Jacques Chirac was elected mayor. In 1981, supported by an unprecedented popular movement, François Mitterand was elected president and spontaneously acclaimed by three million Parisians who, in the middle of the night, invaded the streets, improvising a gigantic ball at the Bastille.

François Mitterand inaugurated the Grands Travaux. "Pharaonic," commented the skeptics: the Quai d'Orsay museum was installed in the Gare d'Orsay, which had been entirely reworked and restored by the Italian Gae Aulenti; and the Grande Arche, the Pyramide du Louvre, the Opéra Bastille, the Bercy quarter, and the Bibliothèque. These are all undoubtedly great works. But they do not always meet with the approval of the Parisians.

Projects abound: from now to the year 2010, no less than five hundred are being carried out. The reorganiza-tion of Place de la Concorde, the construction of Centres de Commerce Internationaux in Bagnolet and in Plaine Saint Denis. The redevelopment of the ancient tenements in Bobigny, Nanterre, and Levallot-Perret, the construction of a third airport in the Paris area, the creation of twelve sports facilities in preparation for the Olympic Games that the city hopes to host in 2008. The new naval port Paris sur Seine at Issy-les-Moulineaux, the complete reorganization of traffic circulation in the urban area, new stations for the TGV trains which, in 2005, will connect most of the large European cities at speeds of over 186 miles per hour.

The dawn of 2000 rose on Paris. The Eiffel Tower shined with a thousand flames of new lights, pro-grammed by computer. A *bateau-mouche* lazily made its way down the Seine, filled with guests for the New Year's Eve ball. It slid toward the future through Paris . . . and two millennia of history.

PARISIAN ARCHITECTURE

STYLE AND STYLES

OF A WORLD'S CAPITAL

The writer Alberto Moravia said that to be in Paris without visiting its landmarks is as foolish as entering a pastry shop when you are on a diet.

This is true, but to visit all of the historical sites in Paris would be utterly greedy. For more than two thousand years, people have built on that strip of land. Paris, along with Rome, is a city that can boast of the greatest number of historical landmarks in the world—four thousand.

You can get lost in the jumble of dates and events that have made the city what it is. You mix up everything: kings, emperors, epochs, and monuments.

And without a guide, just try to distinguish from afar the domes of the Pantheon, the Observatoire, the Invalides, the Académie Français . . . or the Galeries Lafayette!

The history of Paris alternates between strong moments and moments of decline, between tragic and happy events that are inscribed forever on its walls.

Megalomaniac princes left their mark by building palaces and churches; less legible on the walls is the misery of the poor, who rarely had any say about the arrangement of the structures in their city. The monuments were erected to defy time and to be the heritage of future generations; the lopsided houses, made of mud and straw, were destined to disappear almost as quickly as they were built.

So in Paris you find truly beautiful ruins from the ancient Gallic-Roman Lutetia, including the Baths of Cluny and the Arena. Of the people, however, there remains a house, at 3 rue Volta, which dates from just 1292—the oldest house in Paris. The numerous transformations and degradations it has undergone since the thirteenth century only allow us to imagine what the life of its occupants in the Middle Ages might have been. And if it should disappear, the historians have already identified the house of Nicholas Flamel at rue de Montmorency, a mere newcomer from 1407, to succeed it.

But in Paris the past, even if full of history, does not carry weight. You just have to take some precautions in regard to it and always superimpose it on what you see, with the gaze of those who had seen it some centuries before. And then it should not be forgotten that, in Paris, as in Rome—to which it is a kind of twin sister—the ground on which you are walking is not stable. Proof of this is Montmartre, a hill crammed with now-closed quarries that make up an immense gopher's gallery under the *butte*, or knoll. And yet this is what saved it from being covered with high-rise buildings: the ground was not solid enough to support them.

Another example is Notre Dame de Paris, where recently an underground parking lot was to be built, until the subsoil revealed a city predating Caesar's conquest, perhaps Merovingian. What remained of it were pieces of walls, capitols, ceramics, ornaments, and bone, which had been covered by generations of waste material and deposits left by the Seine during its memorable rages.

Since each age has left its imprint on Paris, the city does not have a defined style, as is the case with other old cities like London and Athens. Its style comes from a diversity of styles that were more or less ephemeral, imposed by those who shaped it and those who succeeded in surviving, often by chance, the ravages of time and the mechanical shovel. Therefore, Paris is a city of contradictory signs that reflect, as in a play of mirrors, and provoke the most ardent and surprising architectural correspondences. Seen from below, the Montparnasse tower is a grayish monolith planted right in the middle of a quarter where it does not belong and which was partially destroyed to put it there. Seen from above, it is a spout, a spire that rises in a perfect space and responds from afar to the Eiffel Tower, to the columns of the Place Vendôme and the Bastille, to the Arc de Triomphe, which emerges from the trees of the Champs Elysées, to the Saint Jacques tower, to the Défense, to Sacré Coeur, to the Front de Seine, and to the skyscrapers of the Place d'Italie.

The architecture of Paris fits into time and space. The time is the cement of history that connects the stone of the past to the steel and glass of our day. The space is that eternal space of the Parisian sky, delimited only by the horizon, where the towers of cathedrals rise up like fingers to attract the attention of the gods. Between the two runs a river, which, with its meandering, signs the name of Paris with the most elegant handwriting.

This is why Paris is magical, magical and agonizing. The fact is that, in any part of the city where you find yourself, the eternal is on friendly terms with the ephemeral. The ups and downs of history are only anecdotes in relation to time. The occupation of space is inconsequential in the immensity of the universe. This becomes clear to you at dawn on a summer morning, when the sun comes to caress the severe façade of the Conciergerie and brings tears to your eyes. You forget the Revolution and the unhappy fate of Marie Antoinette. You are simply captivated by the perfect harmony between the place and the moment, between time and space. You have the sensation of a perfect balance between what was, what is, and what will be, between what we are and what we could be, we who modestly pursue elusiveness.

The rest is merely literature.

Moreover, the signs that are the monuments define not only the history of Paris but also the daily life of the Parisians. For them these landmarks are, first of all, points of reference. When it is difficult to find an address, the taxi driver always refers to the landmark that is closest to the address. Behind or in front of the Observatoire, right beside Saint Paul's Church, or "Would you rather go by the Etoile or the Concorde?"

Parisians who adore their city feel as though the monuments have been there from time immemorial. Even in their worst dreams, they cannot imagine that these structures could one day disappear. Yet there was this risk at the time of the Liberation.

In Paris, landmarks could be interchangeable if the legitimacy of their position were not connected to the quarter in which they are found. Place des Vosges is a perfect example of this. This contained space, enclosed in its quadrant, flanked by elegant, proud homes, was not casually created in the Marais. Initially, it was called Place Royale, and Francis I had the idea of building a kind of residential and aristocratic barracks at the city limits, intended to house the officials of his court in luxury. It was Henry IV who completed it, insisting, however, that the private residences leave the ground floor free so that shops could be placed beneath the porticos, a really practical idea to protect pedestrians from the rain and wind. He arranged to have a working class and commercial quarter around the square with the idea of forcing Paris to grow on that side of the Right Bank. Like a good real estate promoter, Henry IV made Parisians leave their eternal Île de la Cité, attracting them to the jousts and organized tournaments in the main, square courtyard that had been transformed into lists. These battles between high-ranking knights were spectacles particularly appreciated by the populace of Paris.

This occasion brought out the entrepreneurs: having visited an area where they were promised larger and more beautiful homes, many Parisians ended up moving there and creating workshops—sometimes small factories—and opening boutiques, progenitors of those that still make the Marais famous. The Place des Vosges is a particularly significant example of social change in Paris. It was a noble square for a century or two, until the populace overflowed the quarters reserved for them and installed themselves in luxurious private residences. For a long time before the Revolution, the proud dwellings of the Place Royale—at that time renamed Place de l'Invisibilité—were transformed into houses and offices. In 1795, it was a disreputable place. In 1860, the quarter was cleaned up and the square took the name Vosgi in homage to the department that had first settled its accounts with the tax office. Victor Hugo moved there in 1826, and subsequently so did Théophile Gautier, Alphonse Daudet, and the actress Rachel. Its public garden was established only in 1866, and the trees were planted in 1872. It would be a pity to settle for a quick visit to this square, which, after all, is relatively calm compared to the nearby streets of Saint Paul, Petit Muse, Birague, Francs-Bourgeois, and Pas-de-la-Mule—all witnesses of the history of the quarter and its origins.

It would be a vain and boring effort to place each landmark in Paris in its historical, symbolic, social, and architectural context. All the monuments of Paris have, more or less, experienced this kind of history.

The Louvre, one of the very first forts in the walls of Paris, was transformed into a royal residence by Charles V. It was abandoned by Louis XIV. It was a prison and place of summary executions during the Revolution, and it is now a museum. The Palais des Tuileries, uncultivated land regularly flooded by the Seine, became a tile factory because the soil was clayey. It was deserted by the workmen, who died from malignant fevers provoked by the pestilence of the river. It was reclaimed by Catherine de' Medici, who had a royal mansion built there independent from the Louvre and then, in 1871, it was burned and sacked by the Communards. Its

stones were purchased by a Corsican family who used them to build a castle in the vicinity of Ajaccio.

The parks and gardens of Paris have equally interesting histories. The park of Buttes-Chaumont was an old gallows transformed into an unhealthy, nauseating public dump and later into a chalk pit. Then, in 1867, Haussmann and Alphand decided to fix it up and turn it into a place for taking walks in order to distract the Paris working class from the nearby taverns on Sundays. Waterfalls, a suspension bridge, grottos, hidden stairs, a temple of love, mountains, and valleys make this park an extraordinary garden, a land of childlike adventures and a completely unexpected place to take a walk in the heart of Paris. Luxembourg Gardens, one of the most beautiful and romantic parks in Paris, visited by Gérard de Nerval, Verlaine, Baudelaire, and Rilke, now hosts the Senate, installed in an old royal palace that inspired the Pitti Palace in Florence. It was a sinister prison during the Revolution, when Jacques-Louis David was locked up there and where he painted his only landscape, which now hangs in the Louvre. The gardens of the Champs Elysées, vegetable gardens at first, were annexed and transformed into ornamental gardens by Catherine de' Medici, the schemer, the bloody queen of the Saint Bartholomew's Day Massacre, who wanted to see something other than rows of peas and carrots from the windows of her room in the Tuileries. The Tuileries garden, designed in the same period as Le Notre, fell into disrepair and became a deserted terrain in the city where the revolutionaries clubbed the aristocrats who attempted to flee, before sending them to the guillotine. In our times, it has once again become a green space vital to the aeration of the capital, where children lead their mothers to walk near the carousels populated by white horses that revolve slowly to the tunes of old songs.

The Parisians adore their parks and their public gardens. Just a hint of spring in the city suffices for them to invade the parks and gardens. Dragging a green stool across the gravel, they sit at the edge of the shade and the sun, remaining enchanted by the fact that it's enough to push open a gate to steal a little happiness from time.

In Paris, you would never finish making an inventory of places and tracing the special stories that all end on the same note, singing the glory of Paris. It is the note that the imperturbable heralds play from the roof of City Hall, their trumpets sounding to the cardinal points the fame of Paris, assisted by grotesque figures and malign monsters that survey the city from above from the towers of Notre Dame, ready to swoop down on anyone who has the courage to speak ill of them.

Paris is a city with a weighty past, respectable and respected; it

has not, however, remained nostalgically petrified in its memories. Sometimes audaciously, nearly always elegantly, Paris has managed to come to terms with its emblematic monuments, protecting them and integrating them into the new dynamic of the city. Paris has become a master in the art of recovery and metamorphosis. It puts its boutiques in old bakery shops, its museums in warehouses and unused stations, its administrations in abandoned palaces, and its technical centers in old slaughterhouses destined for demolition. And with the stones of the Bastille, the Pont de la Concorde was built.

Yet it is also true that Paris knows how to make its inhabitants

feel guilty, knocking down the illusions and the chimeras from the past right before their eyes. All of a sudden, when one of their sacred places is involved, the Parisians are capable of taking up arms. Of course, the sentences of the courts have replaced the guns and the blunderbusses, but the results are the same. The construction projects for the Montparnasse tower, the Beaubourg center, and the Bastille Opéra, which involved destroying entire parts of old Paris—often islands of tottering houses and unhealthy areas needing attention—have provoked outcries, the like of which the capital had not heard since the times of the Commune. They have even been the subject of international consultations.

Of course, Paris has changed. It is in the order of things. At the dawn of the third millennium, to look back nostalgically at a Paris eternally immobile in its history would be vain and ridiculous. And when a Parisian deplores his lost Paris, what he regrets about that time is himself at a period in his life that he feels was happier than now. That which he laments of the old Paris has something of folklore or ghostliness in it. The Parisians of our time have learned to love their city in a different way, without hiding its history—a history that is, after all, eternally inscribed in Paris, a great book of memory open to whoever really wishes to read it.

Since the end of the war, next to the old Paris, a new Paris has grown up, one that has been able to get along with what existed before. The Beaubourg center, with its walkways, conduits, glass

walls, and escalators—which immediately brought it the nickname "Culture Factory"—in the end found its place and has integrated itself into the scenario of the old streets that surround it. The Défense quarter is the prototype of an idealized modern dream city, where visitors will find the Grand Arche, a surprising futuristic creation on the axis of the Arc de Triomphe, the obelisk of the Place de la Concorde, and the pyramid of the Louvre, creates perspectives that stimulate the imagination and invite something more than a mere glance. It is an "arch of triumph," erected to the glory of humanity and a symbol of the hope that, in the future, people can meet each other freely. The whole world goes there already! The Défense is also an open-air museum where, from one esplanade to another, the statues of Joan Miró, Mitroaj, Alexander Calder, Henry Moore, and many other artists of our age put a little color, humor, and poetry into a quarter frequented by hurried businessmen.

The Pyramid of the Louvre, an absolutely transparent glass cap, is a marvelous piece of architecture that magically integrates itself, without contrast, into the frigid scenario of the square courtyard. It is a technological feat that made its architect, I. M. Pei, universally celebrated. The Geode of the Cité des Sciences at Villette, a futuristic ball from Mars or Ganymede, seems to have fallen right in the middle of an area long left abandoned in the wake of a financial scandal that led to the closing of the slaughterhouses of the city.

The Geode is at the heart of a new city where art and technology get along beautifully. Concerts and expositions are held in the Grande Halle at Viande, a memory of Paris preciously preserved in the pavilions consecrated to the architecture of the past that still presents the sketches of a possible or probable future Paris. And the city boasts the new quarter of Bercy and the Omnisport building, a modern pyramid covered with grass car-

peting up to the flat roof. Twenty thousand people can come together here for events like musical comedies, rock concerts, or steeplechase championships. Around it, architects and city planners were able to protect the life of this quarter, which, just a little while ago, had the flavor of a distant province, with its platforms where barrels of wine rolled and its warehouses now transformed into art galleries. The nearby new Ministry of Finance—as severe as a building in which the money of France is counted and cheaters are punished should be—is a building-bridge, half on foundation piles planted in the Seine, which projected the entire quarter into the future. Facing it, the Grande Bibliothèque opens its stone books to the winds of all cultures.

From above, the Front de Seine and Beaugrenelle dominate the old fifteenth arrondissement and are mirrored in the waters of the Seine, where barges full of sand and cement are always passing to be deposited in the ports of Javel or Grenelle. In the evening, when Paris lights up, the towers of the Front de Seine play at being skyscrapers and protecting the little sister of the Statue of Liberty. Here it does not illuminate the world as it does in New York, but rather the tip of the enchanting Isle of Swans, surrounded by the bateaux-mouches. A few steps away is the Eiffel Tower, recently repainted, which shines with all its lights. And you may dream of occupying for one night, one night only, the apartment that Eiffel reserved at the top—and from there to embrace all of Paris.

The Paris of today is a sketch, the trace of a connection between time that has passed and time that does not yet exist.

What will Paris be in the future? The city is keeping that surprise for itself.

For the moment, writers, photographers, and filmmakers enthusiastically bear witness to the Paris of today that, tomorrow, will be the Paris of the past.

82-83 Slim flying buttresses crown the main nave of Notre Dame. The panorama is spectacular: the Ile de la Cité is the true heart of Paris.

83 RIGHT The apse of Notre Dame, designed by Jean Ravy, was built between 1296 and 1330. The central spire is ninety-eight yards high and dates back to the nineteenth century.

84 The incredibly vast space between the nave and the transepts of Notre Dame reflects indefinable echoes, like whispers from the past.

85 Of Notre Dame's three rose windows, the splendid one on the west façade, which is the main one, is the most remarkable from the outside, since the glass seems invisible; at the base of the circumference Our Lady with baby Jesus in her arms receives homage from two archangels.

86-87 The Sainte Chapelle is a Gothic miracle of lightness, brightness, and formal linearity. Built in the thirteenth century by Saint Louis to hold holy relics such as Christ's crown of thorns, the chapel is one of the best achievements of medieval architecture.

88-89 The unmistakable medieval towers of the Conciergerie, covered with sharp slate-clad cones, give an idea of how monumental buildings looked in the thirteenth and fourteenth centuries. The building's sad reputation dates back to the 1789 revolution when, used as a prison, it was considered the anteroom to the scaffold. In the foreground, a perfect *trait-d'union* between the medieval and the Renaissance, Pont Neuf extends toward the Rive Droite.

90-91 Following the direction of the observer's gaze, the Pavillon Khorsabad, Cour Puget, and Cour Marly form an imposing prospect on the north wing of the Cour Napoleon. The last pavilion in the series, with its truncated pyramid roof, held the apartments of Napoleon III.

92-93 The fine network of ornamentation that marks the intervention of Napoleon III illustrates well the eclectic trends that were in fashion at the end of the nineteenth century. It was the last emperor of France who completed, after two and a half centuries, the Louvre that Henry IV had dreamed of.

94, 95, AND 96-97 The Pyramide of the Louvre brusquely interrupts the architectural discourse that brought about the slow conformation of the palatial complex over the centuries. In any case, any addition to the great complex would have been obviously anachronistic. The evening is the best time to admire the work of I. M. Pei, when the complexity of the interior is revealed by artificial light.

98-99 AND 99 RIGHT THE ORIGINS OF THE HÔTEL DE VILLE, PARIS'S OLD TOWN HALL, LIE IN THE FOURTEENTH CENTURY, BUT THE APPEARANCE OF THE BUILDING (REBUILT ON THE ORIGINAL DESIGN AFTER THE FIRE THAT DESTROYED IT IN 1871) DATES FROM THE SIXTEENTH CENTURY, IN THE GLORIOUS DAYS OF FRANÇOIS I.

100 THE RICH GILDING ON THE DÔME DES INVALIDES MAKES THE MEMORIAL CHAPEL, WHICH RECEIVED BONAPARTE'S ASHES IN 1840, VISIBLE AND UNMISTAKABLE EVEN FROM A GREAT DISTANCE.

101 THE ORDERLY COMPLEX OF THE HÔTEL DES INVALIDES, BUILT UNDER THE ORDERS OF THE SUN KING'S GENIAL ARCHITECT, JULES HARDOUIN-MANSART, WAS ORIGINALLY A MILITARY HOSPITAL. INDIRECTLY, THE HUGE SURFACE AREA OF THE COMPLEX IN SOME WAY SUGGEST HOW MANY *INVALIDES* WERE CREATED BY THE WARS FOUGHT BY THE KINGS OF FRANCE.

102-103 REGAL MEDICINE FOR REGAL MELANCHOLY: THE PALAIS DU LUXEMBOURG, WITH ITS *JARDIN*, WAS BUILT TO CURE MARIE DE' MEDICI OF HER HOMESICKNESS FOR TUSCANY. THEN, FOLLOWING THE FATE OF MANY OTHER OPULENT PALACES, WHEN THE HOUR OF THE CONVENTION RANG OUT, IT BECAME A PRISON, WHERE JACQUES-LOUIS DAVID, AMONG OTHERS, WAS A "GUEST."

104 At the top of a column designed closely following the Roman models of Trajan and Adrian, Napoleon Bonaparte continues to watch over Paris from the center of Place Vendôme.

105 Bronze eagles embellish the plinth of the column in Place Vendôme, alluding to the "rapacious" and bellicose attitude of the great soldier who tops the monument.

106-107 Modern sculptures in a temporary exhibit update the street furniture in Place Vendôme. Originally, the square was to hold the statue of Louis XIV, a character who is certainly less popular than the emperor among the Parisians of yesterday and today.

108-109 AND 110-111 THE MIX OF
STYLES OF THE OPÉRA GARNIER,
WHICH IS OFTEN CENSURED BY
CRITICS FOR ITS EXCESSIVE
ORNAMENTATION, SEEMS LIGHT, EVEN
ATTRACTIVE TO THE INEXPERT EYE.
THE BUILDING WAS CONSTRUCTED
UNDER AND FOR NAPOLEON III, WHO
ACTUALLY NEVER HAD THE CHANCE TO
GO TO AN OPERA THERE, DISTRACTED
AS HE WAS BY THE STORM OF THE
FRANCO-PRUSSIAN WAR IN 1870 AND
THE SUBSEQUENT RISING OF THE
THIRD REPUBLIC.

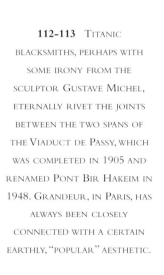

112–113 Titanic blacksmiths, perhaps with some irony from the sculptor Gustave Michel, eternally rivet the joints between the two spans of the Viaduct de Passy, which was completed in 1905 and renamed Pont Bir Hakeim in 1948. Grandeur, in Paris, has always been closely connected with a certain earthly, "popular" aesthetic.

114 AND 115 A Roman-Byzantine triumph in the heart of Montmartre, the Eglise du Sacré Coeur is the second highest point in Paris after the Eiffel Tower. The building, which was built spanning the nineteenth and twentieth centuries, boasts one of the biggest bells in the world.

116–117 IN THE GARDEN OF THE SEVENTEENTH-CENTURY HÔTEL BIRON, HOME TO THE RODIN MUSEUM, A COPY OF THE ILLUSTRIOUS SCULPTOR'S *THINKER* RENDERS ETERNAL THE HUMAN TORMENT OF DOUBT, BEFORE THE DÔME DES INVALIDES.

117 RIGHT SPANNING TWO CENTURIES THAT SAW A LOT OF CONFLICT BUT WERE RICH IN ECLECTIC INSPIRATION, THE PONT ALEXANDRE III AND ITS LOVELY CHERUBS SHOW A REMARKABLE FORMAL CONSERVATISM.

118 AND 119 THE GARE D'ORSAY, INAUGURATED ON JULY 14, 1900, ON THE ANNIVERSARY OF THE STORMING OF THE BASTILLE, AND SAVED FROM DEMOLITION IN 1970, IS NOW ONE OF THE MOST FUNCTIONAL EXHIBITION AREAS IN THE WORLD, DEDICATED TO ART FROM 1848 TO 1914.

120 AND 121 THE UNMISTAKABLE ELEGANCE OF ITS SUMPTUOUS, ENTIRELY GLAZED ROOF IMMEDIATELY MAKES THE GRAND PALAIS STAND OUT IN THE URBAN LANDSCAPE. THE BUILDING, WHICH NOW HOLDS TEMPORARY EXHIBITIONS, IS ONE OF THE MANY MONUMENTS THAT ENRICHED PARIS DUE TO THE VARIOUS UNIVERSAL EXPOSITIONS, IN THIS CASE IN 1900.

122-123 A PECULIAR OBSERVER SEEMS CAPTIVATED, AS USUALLY HAPPENS, IN FRONT OF THE SPECTACULAR VASTNESS OF THE RIVE DROITE BY THE EIFFEL TOWER. IN 1937, THE STATUES THAT POPULATE THE JARDINS DU TROCADÉRO, BY VARIOUS EARLY TWENTIETH-CENTURY SCULPTORS, WERE PLACED IN FRONT OF PALAIS DE CHAILLOT, WHICH WAS BUILT FOR THE INTERNATIONAL EXPOSITION OF THE SAME YEAR.

124 AND 125 THE WORLD WOULD BE DIFFERENT, IN SOME INDEFINABLE WAY, WITHOUT THE EIFFEL TOWER. THE MAGNUM OPUS OF THE ENGINEER GUSTAVE EIFFEL IS SUPERLATIVE IN EVERYTHING: INNOVATION, APPEARANCE, PURE AND SIMPLE BULK, BUT ABOVE ALL BECAUSE IT IS IN THE CONSCIOUSNESS, IT CAN SAFELY BE SAID, OF PRACTICALLY ALL THE CITIZENS OF THE WORLD.

126-127 BETWEEN RIVE DROITE AND RIVE GAUCHE, THE GENTLE CURVE OF THE SEINE SEPARATES PALAIS DE CHAILLOT, WHICH UNFOLDS ITS CURVED WINGS TOWARD PONT D'IÉNA AND CHAMP DE MARS, FROM THE EIFFEL TOWER. THE LATTER, OF COURSE, CANNOT ESCAPE ITS LEADING ROLE AS A TOPOGRAPHIC AND IDEAL FULCRUM: PARIS SEEMS TO REVOLVE AROUND IT.

128-129 In the center of the Défense, the Grande Arche, in the foreground, was opened in 1989. In this grandiose view from the northwest, the structure (116 yards high) responds symmetrically to the Arc de Triomphe, the tiny vanishing point visible at the end of Avenue de la Grande Armée.

129 Created during the 1960s to be Paris's business quarter, la Défense soon outgrew this function and became a sort of huge open-air museum, which, in a forest of eighty ultra-modern skyscrapers, boasts works and street furniture designed by the great names of contemporary architecture.

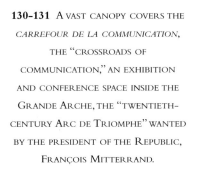

130-131 A vast canopy covers the *Carrefour de la communication*, the "crossroads of communication," an exhibition and conference space inside the Grande Arche, the "twentieth-century Arc de Triomphe" wanted by the president of the Republic, François Mitterrand.

132 AND 132-133 In the area of la Défense, it seems that humanity wants to compete against its own creations and establish new proportions and interactions between itself and the environment. Works such as *La Pouce* ("The Thumb") or the *Tête-Défense* combine sculpture and architecture like reciprocal, direct parameters, intentionally placing the Défense itself at the opposite pole to the Louvre.

134-135 Between the 1970s and 1980s, the fantastic sights of the Forum replaced the enormous covered market of Les Halles, the "belly of Paris." The modern-day structure, developed above- and belowground, reinterprets the area's commercial role in a modern style, with boutiques, restaurants, and bars.

136-137 AND 138-139 IN THE TRADITIONAL, UNIFORM TOWN PLANNING OF THE BEAUBOURG AREA, THE CENTRE POMPIDOU STANDS OUT ALMOST HARSHLY. DUE TO ITS "NEVER BEFORE SEEN" FEATURES, THE BUILDING CAUSED MUCH CONTROVERSY IN THE 1980s. HOWEVER, AS OFTEN HAPPENS, PARIS AND THE WORLD CAME AROUND AND BECAME FOND OF THIS BLOCK OF VISIBLE TUBES AND ESCALATORS.

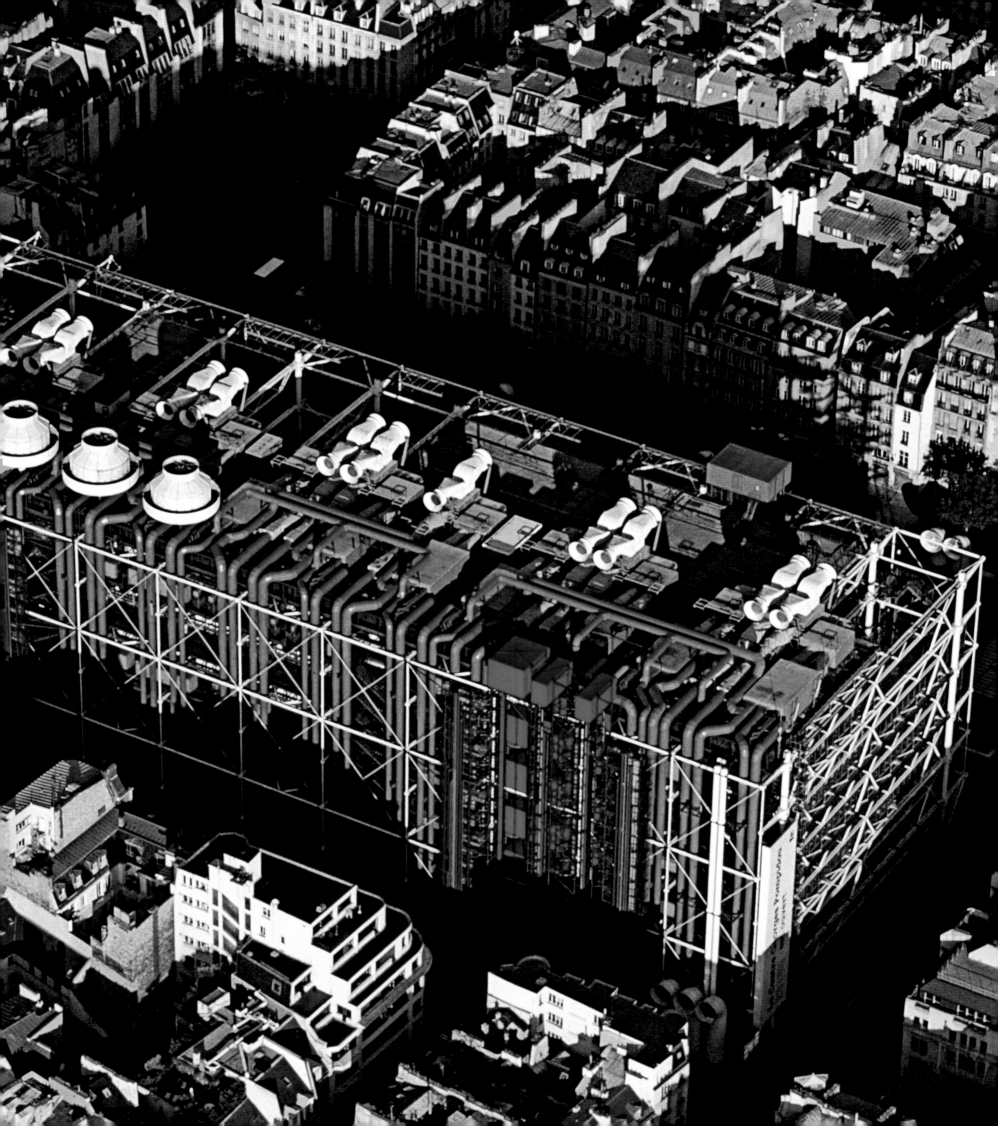

140-141 The Centre Pompidou's scenic escalator is protected by a transparent tube that runs along the façade, on the side of the building facing the square named after the president. The tube itself is arranged in a stepped shape, a sort of playful allusion to its function.

142 and 143 The wonders of the "toy" world created by artists Niki de Saint Phalle and Jean Tinguely appear among the water jets of the Stravinsky fountain, also known as the "Fountain of the Automats." This remarkable work, made in 1982, is near the Centre Pompidou.

144 and 145 The interior of the Centre Pompidou, which can be made complete use of thanks to the "inside out" structure (with the supporting structure, elevators, and tube system on the outside), holds the collections of the National Museum of Modern Art as well as temporary shows.

146-147 The Institut du Monde Arabe stands out for its innovative architecture; it is a museum and cultural center built in 1987 as symbol of the cooperation between France and twenty-one Arab countries. The building's walls have a system of diaphragms to let natural light inside, so as to conserve the objects displayed in the best possible way.

148-149 La Géode houses one of the most spectacular cinemas in the world. Inside the shiny sphere, built in the Cité des Sciences et de l'Industrie at La Villette, films on scientific themes are projected onto a hemispherical screen measuring 1,196 square yards, the biggest in the world.

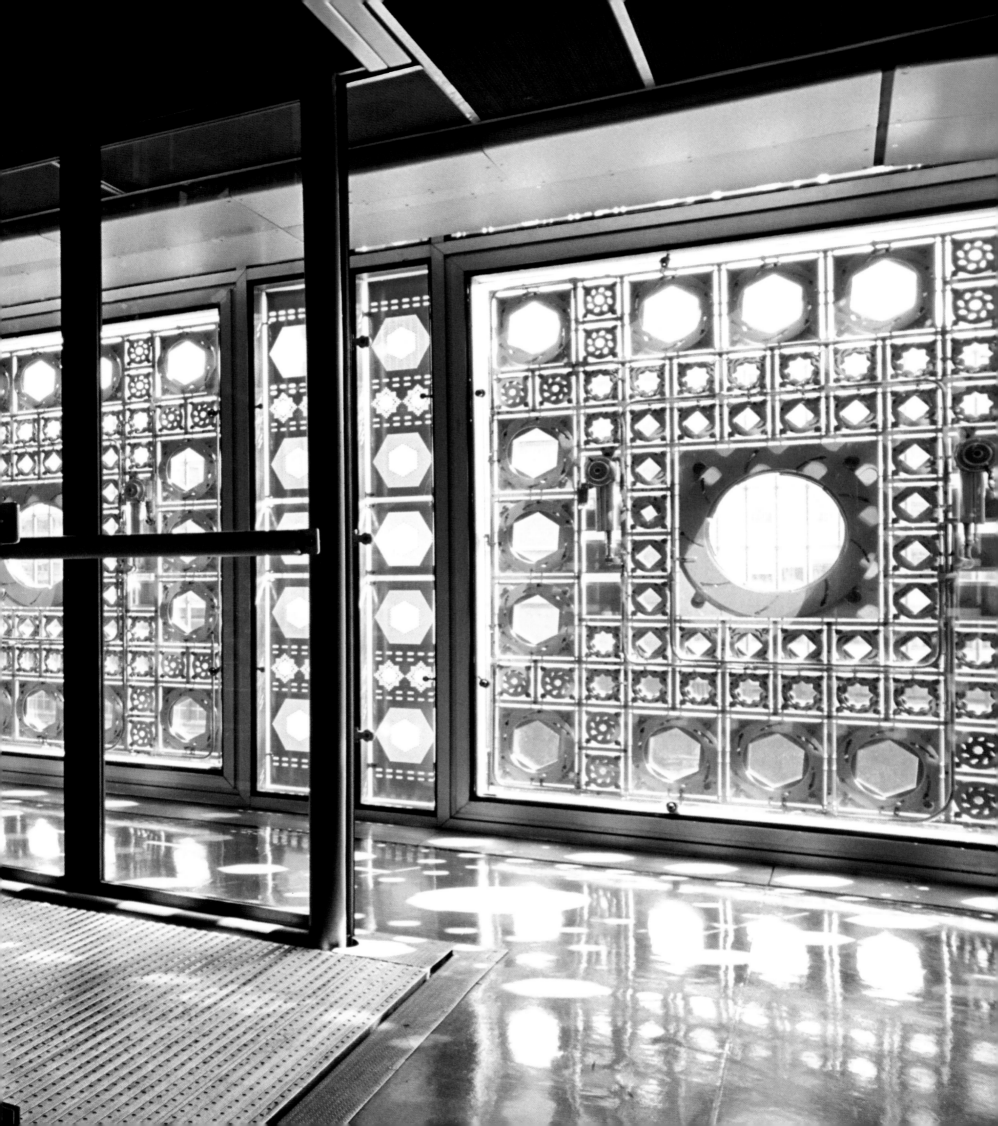

PARIS ADVENTURE

NEW DISCOVERIES
FOR EVERYONE

Paris resembles a tulip bulb whose roots are sunk in the heart of the Seine. The kings of France understood this well and marked the growth of Paris, encircling the city with walls, each time farther from the center, to protect that which they had "grown" with so much effort. In fact, Paris has expanded concentrically; it is not a city to just visit but rather one to peel.

You could start from the outskirts, from the gates of Paris with the flea markets at Vanves, Saint Ouen, Clignancourt, and Montreuil—where many things that no one has wanted for fifty years or so are sold at very high prices—and go toward the center, la Cité.

Or you could start from Notre Dame—and in front of the church square is a plaque inserted in the asphalt that assures you that this is the geographic center of Paris—and then go toward the outskirts of the city.

The only way to get the best out of Paris is to let chance guide your steps. In Paris, there are no itineraries. Or if there are, they are misleading. Only tour guides try to make you believe otherwise.

Paris remains in one's memory as scenes stolen from daily life, furtive images of an intimacy that protects you from indiscreet glances by means of a wisely organized geographic disorder, of extemporaneous meetings with places and people.

The shortest route to knowledge is that of the unknown, sometimes risky, always tempting, and, in Paris, particularly adventurous.

You can easily get lost in Paris. The city has about six thousand streets, blind alleys, boulevards, lanes, avenues, and "mansions" (the private alleys flanked by houses), buildings, quarters, bridges, embankments, crossroads, and paths. It's all a game of hide-and-seek and vaulting horse. The roads turn badly and end in blind alleys or at flights of stairs. They change arrondissements and names without warning. They cross and separate in improbable forks. And they have implausible names: obsolete words, surnames of forgotten people, often unknown even in their own age, and the only memory left is what is written on the street sign.

Indeed, who, even among dyed-in-the-wool Parisians, can say who Honoré-Chevalier was, whose name is given to a street in the sixth arrondissement? He was a baker who, during the Revolution, gave free bread to the needy of the quarter if they presented him with a ticket from the Committee of Public Health; this did not prevent the fine man from being guillotined.

Why is the rue aux Ours called that? There were never any bears in Bear Street. It's just that, in the twelfth century, there was a delicatessen in the street that sold geese—in old French *oues*—which became *ours*, bears, although no one knows why the word was phonetically altered.

Streets have names like Denis Fish, the Fishing Cat, Turn, the White Horse, Pack of Wolves, Mound of Quails, Faithfulness, Dawn Breaking. "With the street names of Paris, one could write poems," said Jacque Prévert.

Think of the imagination required of later administrations who, over two centuries, had to find names for these multitudes of streets, and continue to do so when new ones are created. We can bet that the Commune worker in 1810 who baptized a street of the twentieth arrondissement "China Street" was more concerned about finding a name than about the mysteries of the Middle Empire.

In short, the streets of Paris are malicious and perfidious. They act in a way that causes the people walking them to get lost; they take people where they had no intention of going. *Flâner*, to stroll, is a French word that was created for Paris. In Paris you can walk for hours, always going straight ahead, with your nose in the air, without tiring and, most important, without getting bored. After having

the Louvre is breathtaking. It means trying to sit down to savor the spectacle on a bench, which in theory is reserved for tired visitors but which vagabonds have ancestral rights to, renegotiated daily by a good-natured guard. Would you prefer to go on a tangent? Passing over the Saint Michel bridge, you reach Saint Germain and the swarm of streets around the cafés where students and fashionable writers have their breakfast. These include the welcoming terraces of the Brasserie Lipp, the Deux Magots, the Flore, the Rhumerie Martiniquaise, or the Café de la Mairie, which, as the only authorized tavern on Place Saint Sulpice, has the exclusive right to sell petits crèmes and large draft beers. And why not go along the river? There you meet fishermen, though there are no longer many of

them. Once a year they meet for a competition on the banks of the Seine. From there, when they have a bit of luck or they come upon a hysterical fish with suicidal tendencies, they pull out a minuscule inedible goby, which they throw back into the water after the ritual photo. There you also meet the lovers who, since they have been embracing there for centuries, have bent the trees in the direction

wandered around, at the end you can always find a Métro to tell you where you are. Although Paris is a city that is expert in confusing its latitudes and longitudes, it is very easy to be a pedestrian there. And this is perfectly fitting because, when all is said and done, walking is the only way to draw close to the city and discover its workings. So let's set off!

We start from Notre Dame, an immense vessel planted right in the heart of Paris, and we go toward . . .

Toward what? Shall we go straight on? That means ending up on the point of the Vert Galant from where the view of the Seine and

of their kisses. Or you could turn sharply to the right to cross the Seine by the Notre Dame bridge, and in passing greet the flower sellers of the Quai aux Flores, solid as the Pont Neuf, who offer roses and lilacs. And then you would cross the quarter of Saint Paul, haunt of the antique dealers and secondhand sellers, and approach the Bastille from the Place des Vosges.

That is, unless you decide to go to the left, which obliges you to walk toward the National Assembly, strolling through proud quarters with their doors carefully barred. From there you would go toward the Eiffel Tower and, crossing a bridge (whichever you like—there

are five or six), you go over the Seine to reach the Right Bank, the chic side, where there are luxurious boutiques and fashionable designers. A choice worthy of Corneille! In any case, whatever you choose, don't settle for walking with your eyes on the ground or prudently raised to the level of the traffic lights. Look up! Look at the balconies and the hanging gardens that spill over the terraces at the tops of buildings. Dream in front of the iron gates where cats, hidden in the tree branches, take the place of birds posed on the foliage of other trees, and this since Brandt modeled them a hundred years ago. Let yourself be surprised by the giants, the nude women, the baskets of flowers, the caryatids, and the heads of gorgons that adorn the façades and survey the street. Let yourself be moved by that rose bush, that bunch of weeds, even that tree, born of a seed, abandoned by a bird, that germinated blindly in the crack of a wall. Go farther up toward that blue curvature of zinc roofs and the iridescent color of the sky. It lights up the ground.

The Paris sky is the most beautiful in the world. Whether it is blue or gray or adorns itself with the iridescent colors of the passing clouds, it is unique. The summer sky clothes the city with soft blue at the first light of dawn and hardens during the day, slowly darkening until the evening, when it becomes violet and blends with carmine and gold mixed together. The rainy sky summons more lightning than thunder and creates puddles of light on the wet pavement. A spurt of Chinese ink suddenly splits to let in opalescent glimmerings of clarity from above. The snowy sky, like a blanket tucked in around the city, brushes the roofs and suddenly, with the lightness of a butterfly's wing, whitens the roads, the benches, the parapets, and the bridges and sits on the window ledges. The sky of Paris takes on the color of the time that passes.

Paris is a theatrical performance with only one setting, the city, and four acts—spring, summer, autumn, and winter. In April, right from the first rays of reflected sun, the horse chestnuts become colored with a gouache tonality and take on the air of a distant forest. The waiters in the cafés put down the awnings over the terraces to protect the Neapolitan cassatas, and women show off dresses with skirts that look like flower petals gently overturned on the pavement. A divine month, August, in Paris! How beautiful the city is when it's deserted—beautiful and easy, compliant. At six, the sun rises perpendicular to the Seine, which makes melted gold flow. The city, spattered with gold, lazily awakens. The sky fills with gulls that fly over the slow moving rows of towboats. On Pont Mirabeau, a student leans out over the water. At ten in the evening, as the sun disappears behind Notre Dame, a mauve sunset rises from the river under a streaked sky. A tugboat, croaking, turns toward the sea, slowly pulling the night behind it at the end of its cable. The first Monday of September: the Parisians jam the highways, jam Paris, and, despite the police who play at directing the scene, the waves of cars, at high tide, flow over onto the sidewalk. The sky turns pearl gray. The trees turn red. The air is so sweet that you could bathe in it. And it is already December. The Seine drags its lead-colored waters, striped here and there from the glow of the lamps. The night arrives quickly. The light runs along the neon signs. The Parisians breathlessly run from one shop to another: rue Lafayette, Chaussée d'Antin, rue de Rennes. And when the city is sleeping, the sulky buildings seem to bend their shoulders.

The sky is like a sheet over the roofs of Paris. These roofs resemble a bluish ocean, a hurrying wave that fills the horizon, where the dome of a church and the horses of the Grand Palais sail, eternally soaring toward a sky that they will never reach.

The roofs of Paris! Mimi Pinson, the Parisian sketched by Alfred de Musset, opens the window on the light of an evening in the summer, waters the geraniums arranged carefully on the window sill and feeds the stray cats, tight-rope walkers of the highest level, plucked for an instant from the usual worries of their risky vagabond existence. The roofs of Paris hide secrets. Each house has its story, which tells of the greatness and the decadence of a marshal of the Empire, of a chaplain of the court, of the life and death of a poet or a painter, of the joys and sorrows of anonymous people everywhere.

A Parisian easily ignores this flood of slate, tiles and zinc that covers the city, unless, of course, he lives under those roofs.

Which is always better than living under the bridges.

And, in this regard, in Paris, you need to know how distinguish between the bridges where people sleep and the riverfronts where people take walks.

By day, under the bridges of Paris or near them, under the shade of the poplars, some blessed souls who do not know about punching a time-card, watch the barges—and time—pass by. Stretched out on a newspaper or an old potato sack supplied by a generous coal seller (one can be a vagrant and nevertheless maintain a certain level of comfort), their heads delicately raised in the direction of a bottle neck, they admire—with eyes half shut in a fake sleep—the legs of the beautiful foreigners in ecstasy over the barges moored for a night or for a lifetime, which speak of wandering and a world without borders. At night, under the bridges, they sleep. The banks, instead, serve the lovers of Paris who make the Seine their bed.

At the riverfronts, people meet each other and sometimes clash with each other, both tourists and residents, without distinction as to race or language. From one part of the Seine to the other, the riverfronts of Paris are like Ali Baba's cave. The used-book sellers have been installed there for centuries. From large green stalls that carpet the bulwarks, they offer the passersby treasures from the attics of bankrupt publishers or from collectors whose progeny didn't know what to do with all those piles of old paper half eaten by mice. Everything is held together in a tentative way by plaster of Paris paperweights of the busts of Hugo, Voltaire, or Rousseau. The Parisians adore their used-book sellers to the point that when it was rumored some years ago that their stalls would be closed, all of Saint Germain mobilized to bar the police. An agreement was quickly reached: only the opening and closing hours and the days of the week that the stalls would be closed were established. On those days, the bulwarks are used by Parisians to chain their bicycles.

The booksellers along the riverfront, like the watercolorists of Montmartre, are an integral part of the life and panorama of Paris.

Who today could believe that Montmartre, just one hundred years ago, was a hill covered with fruit trees, vines, some sheds, and a good forty mills? Now the Basilica of the Sacred Heart (Sacré Coeur), which the Parisians call "Chantilly cake" (the postcard of this monument is a big seller), protects the painters of the Place du Tertre and even the shameless pleasures of the rue Pigalle. A little secret about Paris that few Parisians know: the Sacré Coeur was built with the stone of Chateau-Landon, which, as an effect of rainwater, secretes a white substance similar to paint. You shouldn't be surprised, then, by the immaculate color of the basilica; the more it rains, the whiter it becomes.

As to the painters of the square who portray the willing tourists one after the other, it remains to be seen if among them there will be a new Renoir, Braque, Picasso, Matisse, Dali, or Toulouse-Lautrec, all of whom lived and worked there.

Parisians don't go up to Montmartre; they find it dull. Or perhaps they are too lazy to climb the six hundred steps that lead to the basilica, the highest point in Paris, which culminates at 152 yards. The hill of Montmartre is, for Parisians, a kind of Annapurna. You can bet that since 1914, the year in which the basilica was inaugurated, they discovered a less tiring way to reach the "seventh heaven"—namely a funicular railway. But evidently that was not enough for the Parisians.

So much the worse for the citizens who don't know that Montmartre is extraordinarily fascinating, with its stone-paved alleys, furrowed old houses, flowering interior courtyards, old lamps, wobbly ivy-covered walls, secret paths, and wild gardens clinging to the hill, which have somehow been able to withstand the pickaxes of the real estate entrepreneurs. Montmartre is *la bohème*. It is the impudence of the little rascal; the insolence of Gavroche, the urchin in Victor Hugo's *Les Misérables*; the cheek of the Parisian boy humorously drawn by Poulbot. And it is also the memory of the windmills whose arms protect lovers. Of those famous mills, only one remains, at the cemetery of Montmartre.

All the cemeteries of Paris are history books, closed forever more. The aristocratic cemetery of Passy is the resting place of numerous people guillotined during the Revolution; on their tombs are inscribed the great names of France. The cemetery of Saint Blaise is a tiny bucolic enclave near the oldest church in Paris, the one from which pilgrims departed for Santiago de Compostela. The secret graveyard of Calvaire opens only once a year, on November 1, from 8 A.M. to 6 P.M.; it is true that, for some time now, there have not been descendents who can bring flowers to the tombs of the Merovingians that the cemetery hosts. The cemetery of Père-Lachaise is a world apart—it is a vast, romantic, silent garden where you need a map to get around (available for free at the entrance). It is where the dates and

and certainties are shattered. At the cemetery of Père-Lachaise, there has been an invasion of statues, and not all of them have a good reason for being there. Perhaps they were put there when no one was looking, or because they couldn't be placed elsewhere. There are thousands of statues in Paris: a whole population of bronze and marble that lives in the squares, at the crossroads, in street corners, in public gardens, along the long stairways that lead to official buildings. And when there is no other place, they are put at the tops of columns, on the façades of buildings, and even on the roofs. There were even more before the war, but the Germans took down several of them and sent them to foundries where they were turned into cannons, which, since then, have had the time to get rusty. For Parisians, anything can be

transformed into a statue—famous men and unknown men, feelings, states of mind, myths, and ideas. Sometimes these statues are surprising, such as César's famous centaur, made of bolts, rags, and broom handles cast in bronze and placed right in the middle of the Latin Quarter. Or they leave you dumbfounded, such as Buren's truncated columns in the garden of the Palais Royale, to which the Parisians, not finding an artistic reason for their existence, attributed these functions:

the epitaphs cry out, creating a balance between anonymous and famous people. Those celebrities that one could hardly approach alive are there, attentive and available, now that they have eternity ahead of them. At Père-Lachaise, after visiting Colette, Alfred de Musset, Frédéric Chopin, Edith Piaf, Amedeo Modigliani, Guillaume Apollinaire, Oscar Wilde, Yves Montand, Marcel Proust, Molière, Jim Morrison, and Abelard and Heloise, united for all eternity, you should stop, if only for a minute, in front of the blank wall where, with no more breath or ammunition, the last of the Communards fell in 1871 under the attacks of MacMahon. Paris has its wailing walls where its illusions

"perches for birds, stools for children, lampposts for dogs."

In most cases, the statues of Paris are emotional: the Marshals of the Empire who stand guard on the façade of the Louvre; the Queens in Luxembourg Gardens; the Statue of Liberty—a replica in miniature of the one given by France to New York—that illuminates Paris from the tip of the Isle of Swans; the Balzac by Auguste Rodin that seems to be directing traffic at the corner of boulevard Raspail; the four Graces symbolizing the cities of France, set on the pavilions in the Place de la Concorde (Juliette Drouet, who was Victor Hugo's lover, was the model for one). And how could you, unless

you have a hard heart, not fall in love with Aristide Mailliol's beauties, who sleep nude, summer and winter, in the gardens of the Tuileries and dream of the shores of the Mediterranean where they were born.

The streets of Paris lead everywhere and to all the countries in the world. Streets are named after Rome, Danzig, London, Saigon, Madagascar, and New York. There is a Cairo passageway and squares named after Mexico, Italy, Stalingrad, and Warsaw. They even lead to ancient Greece—to Montparnasse. However, all the streets of the world also lead to Paris. Certainly because of the Montparnasse railroad station and its departure and arrival tracks, but especially because of the students of the eighteenth century who recited their second-rate verses there and dedicated the place to the Greek poets.

Montmartre is the popular *bohème*; Montparnasse is the chic *bohème*. You see that clearly, wandering around the streets of the quarter where artists' ateliers—comfortable, on two floors, sublimely lit from the north by immense windows—are hidden in blind alleys with flowers, carefully protected by digital number codes. Today not many artists remain, but in the early to mid-1900s, it was the privileged haven of poets, musicians, writers, and political refugees. Lenin and Trotsky lived in Montparnasse. After the Second World War, it was the Americans who had success in Montparnasse. But it has to be said that Ernest Hemingway, Henry Miller, Gertrude Stein, Man Ray, Ezra Pound, and the others perhaps came to Paris more to flee the prudish America of those days and to benefit from the decreased cost of the pleasures of Paris—the rate of exchange of the dollar was already most interesting—than to paint or write. The Lost Generation left a lot of money in the banks of the quarter, to the point that a copper tag at the Closeries des Lilas indicates the table that Hemingway occupied. Like other struggling emigrant artists—Soutine, Foujita, Zadkine, Marc Chagall, Paul Klee—the Americans produced some masterpieces: *Quiet Days in Clichy, A Moveable Feast*, among others. There is a certainty that something of our times was played out there, between the Dôme and the Coupole in the cigar smoke and the alcohol and the trepidation of jazz. Paris is a feast, a perpetual feast that is perennially restarted. Speaking of feasts, the Parisians have an innate sense of improvisation. At the end of the 1990s, the prefecture of the police went through agony a number of times attempting to impede whoever was holding the famous White Nights. The game was simple: one afternoon, preferably in the summer, the address of a place kept secret up until the last moment circulated around Paris at the speed of sound. This was where people would meet as soon as night fell. In general, it was a well-known location in Paris: Place Vendôme, de Füstenberg, or Dauphine, the footbridges of the Arts or rue Saint Louis-en-l'Île. By the magic of cell phones, the address was communicated only at the very last moment, and the challenge consisted of being at that place at the specified time, neither earlier nor later. In the precise moment in which the bells of the quarter rang the time of the appointment, hundreds of cars, from out of nowhere, blocked traffic. The drivers took folding chairs and camping tables out of their trunks, which they arranged elegantly with provisions and bottles. There, in the open air, in the most beautiful places in Paris, they improvised a dinner for two hundred to three hundred people who, a few hours earlier, didn't know each other and who were now sharing foie gras, champagne, and liqueur. To the great joy of the residents of the area, they were quite often invited to the feast! By the time the police arrived on the scene, everyone had disappeared, leaving not a trace, not even a soiled piece of paper!

Parisians are facetious, impertinent, irreverent, and willingly inclined to mockery. In a word, they are free. The winds of freedom sometimes change into a gale or even into a blizzard; the history of Paris is full of these storms, unexpected and uncontrollable, which have shaped the city and the personality of its inhabitants. It's what is called the "air of Paris." That air that, as the poet Paul Verlaine felt, gives spirit to those who have none.

CHAUMET
PARIS

160–161 The juxtaposition of opposites— antique/modern, classic/innovative—often underlies the philosophy with which jewelry is considered.

162 AND 163 In semidarkness or in bright light, fleeting images emerge here and there in the discreet cosmos of Parisian cafés: details from another era, white caps and fin de siècle suits throw back the echo of a dreamy past, which never really ended.

164 AND 165 Marking the boundary between the surface and the subterranean worlds, the metro entrances in central Paris show off beautiful wrought-iron work. However, the attractive decorations do not date from the early twentieth century, as the Art Deco style would suggest, but from the 1970s: the reference is to the actual age of the first underground line, which opened in 1900.

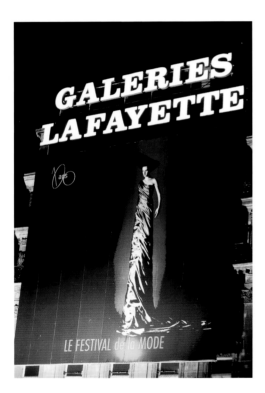

166 AND 167 A FIRST-RATE THEATER OF REFINED CONSUMERISM, THE GALERIES LAFAYETTE (WHOSE NAME DERIVES FROM THE STORE'S FIRST LOCATION, BETWEEN CHAUSÉE D'ANTIN AND RUE LAFAYETTE) STILL RETAINS THE ENORMOUS GLASSED DOME FROM THE EARLY TWENTIETH CENTURY. THE GRANDIOSE ATMOSPHERE IS STILL THE SAME: THIS IS THE AGORA OF SHOPPING, WHICH INFLUENCED THE WORLD.

168 AND 169 Another type of solemnity emanates from the nineteenth-century reading room of the Bibliothéque Nationale (12 million books are kept here), which is immersed in silence and interspersed with slender columns that emphasize the vastness of the room.

170 AND 171 On tiptoe at the Opéra Garnier: ballerinas from the legendary Moscow Bolshoi prepare for the show.

172-173 The symphony of Paris, among elaborate ornamentation and ranks of severe columns, is often unexpectedly enriched by the notes of "street music," which is not at all intimidated by the pomp and splendor of history.

174 AND 175 Emotions carved out and sought out in sculpture: a weeping statue on the tomb of Richelieu in the Chapelle de la Sorbonne, and a visit to the statue collections of the Louvre.

PAVILLON SULLY

176 AND 177 *Coronation of Napoleon and Josephine* by Jacques-Louis David; *Freedom Guides the People*, by Eugene Delacroix. It's not hard to get carried away by history in the halls of the Louvre museum.

178 AND 179 Pont Neuf, which was "new" when it was opened in 1607, crosses the river at the westernmost tip of Ile de la Cité.

180-181 Acrobatic, anonymous scribblers, battling against grayness and uniformity, constantly update corners and views of Paris, especially where stations, railway bridges, and trains are concerned. Pont Bir Hakeim is no exception, even if the municipal whitewashers occasionally wipe out this ephemeral graffiti.

182-183 CAPRICIOUS PARIS OFTEN RELIES ON THE INSTABILITY OF THE WEATHER TO SHOW OFF ITS CHANGEABLE BEAUTY TO FULL EFFECT. THE SPECTACLE OF PONT ALEXANDRE III, PERHAPS THE LOVELIEST IN THE CITY, TAKES ON DRAMATIC TONES, WITH STATUES APPEARING TO COME TO LIFE AND SHAPES DEFINED BY DEEP SHADOWS.

184-185 IN THE EVENING, THE THEATER OF LIFE LIGHTS UP IN ATTIC WINDOWS, WHICH PLAY SUCH A GREAT PART IN CREATING PARIS'S ALLURE. TOWERING OVER EVERYTHING, THE EIFFEL TOWER CONFIRMS THE IMPRESSION OF FAMILIARITY GIVEN BY THE FAMOUS "ROOFTOPS OF PARIS": A CITY ABOVE A CITY, HELD UP BY ROMANTIC PRINCIPLES.

186-187 AND 188-189 Just opposite the Ile de la Cité, the stalls selling used books and prints on Quai Saint Michel, like the bookstores on rue de la Boucherie, are among the favorite destinations of book lovers all over the world. For those tempted by the smell of printed paper, these dusty havens are sure to hold surprises and excitement.

190 "Used" doesn't mean inferior: booksellers around the Ile de la Cité offer not only masses of interesting LIVRES DE POCHE from decades ago, but also weighty and precious centuries-old tomes.

191 An antiques shop offers a pleasant and unexpected encounter with holiness: an effigy of Saint Michael makes a gesture of blessing to the road reflected in the window.

192-193 In Paris you can turn the corner and walk into fairy-tale worlds come true: such is the art of murals, in this case on rue Max Dormoy.

194 **LEFT** Architectural scenery in multiple styles overlaps, creating the varied stage of rue Saint Michel.

194 **RIGHT** A slightly melancholy and nonchalant joie de vivre is in perfect tune with Paris and the Parisians, for example on the notes of a pianola.

FROM 195 TO 199 Many of the slightly mad bohemian painters of the seventeenth and eighteenth centuries lived and died around Place du Tertre. This is still an "artsy" area today, lived in and frequented by artists, collectors, and browsers who often have their portrait done, won over by the skill of a more or less well-known lucky artist. Montmartre is an excellent diversion from the "bigger" Paris with its big history, big monuments, and big traffic.

200 AND 201 ENNOBLED BY THE NAME *BROCANTAGE*, THE JUNK-DEALING BUSINESS IS AN IMPORTANT ELEMENT IN THE ECONOMY OF THE PARISIAN DREAM. WITH THEIR MARKETS STUFFED FULL OF EVERYTHING, CLIGNANCOURT, VANVES, AND MONTREUIL ARE THE STOPS ON AN EXCITING JOURNEY THROUGH A WORLD IN WHICH HISTORY IS DESCRIBED BY MINUTE OBJECTS, EVERYDAY ITEMS, AND THINGS FROM DAYS LONG GONE: TIME, IN THESE DUSTY SHOPS, DOESN'T HOLD MUCH POWER.

PARIS AS TIME PASSES

One of the best stories about Paris is set at the Saint Ouen flea market.

Nineteen forty-two. Paris was occupied. The Serpette market at Saint Ouen opened only once a week, Sunday, and received more sellers than buyers. The Parisians, to survive, tried to sell everything that was sellable at the *marchés aux puces,* the flea markets. One day a junk dealer stopped in front of a gypsy planted on the sidewalk next to an old disassembled carousel, a pile of misshapen wood that made a miserable figure in the rain. The junk dealer stopped, rummaged rapidly through the pile and offered a price, which the gypsy accepted without arguing, quite content to rid himself of the wet, decrepit wood, not even good for burning. The junk dealer promised to return after a half hour with the money and two porters to load the wood into a pushcart. The seller waited patiently. A second junk dealer arrived and he, too, was interested in that disassembled carousel. He asked the price and, without getting ruffled, the gypsy answered that the carousel had already been sold and that the buyer would be returning with the amount agreed upon. Well, then, said the dealer, if it has not been paid for, that means it's still for sale! Nothing doing, said the gypsy. My word is my word. And even if a man can raise the price, offer double, five times, ten times as much as the first pays, nothing doing. With his fists in his pockets, the gypsy, not giving up, waited for the customer who had given his word.

The first junk dealer returned after several hours. The gypsy was still there,

standing stoically in the rain. He took his money and without a word turned on his heels and disappeared.

Nineteen forty-six. The war had ended. One Sunday morning, a well-to-do gentleman went to see the administrator of the flea market and asked him if he remembered a certain gypsy who, during the war, had sold him an old carousel. A gypsy? There are a hundred around here. You can find one there, if he's still there. After wandering around for hours in a rough and dirty terrain cluttered with broken carriages, the man found his gypsy, sitting and calmly smoking his pipe under the roof. "Are you the one who sold me a old carousel with wooden horses four years ago?"

"Why? Doesn't it work? Anyway I don't intend to reimburse you."

"Oh, yes, it's fine! No, better than fine. I just came to give you the balance of what I owe you."

"You don't owe me anything. You already paid me."

"Paid, yes, but not at the price it was worth. I saw that all the panels of your carousel were painted by Toulouse-Lautrec. I resold them in America for a thousand times more than I paid you. I came to share the profits with you."

Stories like this circulate by the thousands in the flea markets at the gates of Clignancourt, Vanves, and Montreuil. Obviously, nowadays you are unlikely to find a Picasso at a ludicrously low price on the stall of the rag seller or a junk dealer. The chic antique dealers from rue Jacob or Faubourg Saint Honoré have already passed through—the "fleas" get up early.

On Saturdays, at five o'clock in the morning, armed with flashlights, international antique dealers come here to resupply themselves with objets d'art. The trucks arrive from everywhere and the *puciers* begin to show their things. It is a real jungle, and you have to have an expert eye to identify a Daum from the 1930s under an incredible layer of filth or an eighteenth-century engraving spotted with mold.

Beginning at seven, the market "legally" opens, and then it is a picturesque kermis where you go from stand to stand, a cone of fried potatoes in your hand, to discover bizarre objects or an authentic work of art. Each week, on Saturday, Sunday, and Monday, two hundred thousand visitors skim the hundreds of lanes of the thirteen Saint Ouen markets followed by fortune-tellers in flying skirts and illegal peddlers trying to sell off objects of a sometimes dubious origin. The terraces of the small bistros where they serve *moules marinière* by the ladle are thronged as much by cus-

tomers as by sellers of roses and guitar players, clones of Django Reinhardt, who have only three days each week to pass their hat around this crowd. In this good-natured atmosphere, you look for an ivory cigarette holder, an African mask from the beginning of the nineteenth century (imported the week before from an atelier that mass-produced them in the Ivory Coast), a batch of lace, a signed piece, a rare piece of furniture or a painting by a master—always hoping to have gotten it for nothing from a merchant who knew nothing, or who pretended to know nothing about the object. Often you leave with the feeling of having made a good deal. You always learn something, even if it isn't necessarily useful for daily life. So you feel a little more cultured when you know that, until the eighteenth century, bathtubs were made of copper, that ebony from Makassar should be cleaned with milk, or that the corsets of the ladies of the Second Empire had fifty-four holes to be laced.

Flea markets are really the proof that our age is forgetful and versatile, since it passes, without transition, from amnesia to infatuation. The Saint Ouen fleas have launched many decor styles. The style of Henry III and the first baroque period, destined to end in the fireplaces, was revived here. Art Déco, Art Nouveau, the Napoleon III style, the furnishings of the 1930s, the ceramics of Keramis, the glasswork of

Gallé—the 1950s and then the 1960s have come around again.

And all this in only a hundred and fifty years.

Saint Ouen was born in 1841. At that time, Adolphe Thiers, president of the council, decided to ring Paris with fortified walls that would separate the city from the suburbs. The fortifications disappeared to make space for the large ring road. On the other side of this wall, you found the "zone," a kind of no-man's-land, inhabited by a miserable population that lived on what it recovered from the garbage of the well-off quarters. The Parisians had the habit of coming here to purchase objects at the lowest prices, especially furniture, often imperfect, but something that could be fixed and repainted and used again.

So we know how the fleas were born, but we are not too sure of the origin of the name. It is said that it was Thiers himself, coming one day to visit the area and seeing from the top of the fortifications that pile of heterogeneous objects of iron, of rags, who exclaimed: "But this here is the meeting place of the fleas!" Others propose more of a mattress-maker version for the term. In any case, the name has made its fortune given that we find it in many languages, all around the world.

The Saint Ouen market today is the largest attic in the world. In a few hours here, you can go around the world several times and skip from century to century and experience the infinity of human dreams. It is a gigantic place, highly controlled and very safe, frequented by Parisian high society. It is not unusual to cross paths with film stars, famous writers, and politicians that you have seen that very morning on television. Perhaps they come to meditate on the precariousness of glory in front of the cracked lifeless busts of plaster or bronze of individuals once famous and now completely forgotten, who have ended up here in the middle of the odds and ends and dusty objects.

All of Paris goes to the flea markets with an infantile soul and the feeling of participating in a treasure hunt. The phenomenon is not recent. As early as the 1930s, Matisse found here his celebrated African mask, and André Breton, the pope of surrealism, made the flea markets his favorite walk on Sunday afternoons. Breton was not interested in the pecuniary value of things and wasn't trying to make an investment when he bought a spoon with holes, which, it was said, Verlaine had used for his absinthe, or the canvas of Sunday painter unknown to the world. It was said, however, that recently a brownish daub that belonged to him was knocked down at an exorbitant price during a famous auction of his personal objects.

Breton said about all the junk he collected: "They are things that you do not find elsewhere, unusable, broken, incomprehensible, and often perverse, but they have the power to remind us of people that we have never known."

The little history of Paris lies at the bottom of the laundry baskets of its flea markets. All those objects, put on display, sold as charms, are the latest words of stories of which we can never know the beginnings, stories that you have all the time in the world to invent, following your own imagination.

Objects dream. And looking at them, you dream with them. You find yourself elsewhere. In the past. And you let yourself be taken by the melancholy of passing time, secretly regretting that it, too, goes at excessive speeds.

204-205 AND 206-207

CROWDED STALLS OFFER AN INCREDIBLE JUMBLE OF VARIED CHARACTERS AND OBJECTS. SYMBOLS AND DREAMS MATERIALIZE IN THIS MULTICOLORED CHAOS: YOU NEED A GOOD EYE TO DIG UP THE "RARE FIND," BUT OCCASIONALLY SOME LUCKY SOULS HAVE COME ACROSS TRUE MASTERPIECES.

THE CITY OF GRANDEUR

PARIS

GOURMAND

Imagine that you are crossing this magnificent Paris, in a hurry to go to the Eiffel Tower or the Louvre when, suddenly, at the end of the street, at the exit of the Métro, you come upon a place outside of time, overflowing with colors, odors, laughter, and shouting—a Parisian market.

At first sight, that pedestrian zone protected by uniform green roofing that occupies the width of the street or the center of a square seems like all the other markets in the world. But you enter and the atmosphere changes. On the counters placed side by side is a mixture of colors and odors. Pyramids of fruit, boxes of vegetables, stacks of cheese, rosaries of sausages, armfuls of peonies, fish artistically arranged on beds of crushed ice decorated with algae. Wafting over everything are the fragrances of roast chicken and bread fresh from the oven. And in an indescribable chaos punctuated by the thunder of the frying pan and casserole salesmen positioned at strategic points, you play the matador, trying to avoid overloaded baskets, shopping carts, and baby carriages. The salesmen shout to the regular customers who are undecided or indifferent.

The picturesque scene, the quickness of the popular spirit, the poetry of the Parisian markets—you have to immerse yourself, participate in the freedom of tone, of laughter, of anecdote, of gesture, and sharpen your vocabulary and fluency. You have to profit from this exceptional place, crucible of culture, tastes, and ideas where all of Paris meets, meets and congratulates itself without animosity. Politicians know this so well that they come here to look for their potential supporters. They shake the hands of perfect strangers as if they were close relatives. They embrace dignified old women, who will have some-thing to talk about in the evening at the family dinner table. They pat the heads of youngsters, who occasionally take advantage of the situation to rummage through their pockets.

It would take a book to list all the markets in Paris. There are twelve covered and sixty-two open-air markets that operate every day of the year, rain, wind, or snow. Each arrondissement has one or more markets, each with its own specialty, its own character, and its own picturesque characters: Saint Charles, Belgrand, Batignolles, Mouffe, and so on. One of the oldest, the Montorgueil market is, with its fifty stalls, all that remains of Les Halles, the old general market, which until 1969 was the largest food market in the world. Émile Zola called it "the belly of Paris" and gave an almost naturalistic description of it. It was an anxious quarter that, from dawn till dusk, functioned with its rhythm, its laws, its culture, its colorful language, and its propensity to revolt. Here was born the folklore of the popular *Parisien* and his gallery of portraits immortalized forever: big men solid as oxen, great workers and ready to fight; termagants with arrogant language and nearly savage flower sellers; police in long coats and sharp street urchins; butchers' boys with roguish tendencies who, after work, danced to the sound of the accordion with the high-society ladies in beaded evening gowns who came to cure their hot flashes with the popular dances of the rue des Vertus. Today, if the heart is still there, the stomach is instead elsewhere: at Rungis, on the road to the Orly airport. Rungis is as big as the principality of Monaco, where the covered markets are the size of soccer fields, visited daily by twenty thousand buyers served by six thousand sellers! Monetary transactions have reached levels such that twenty banks have opened offices there. A gigantic thing, worthy of Rabelais.

212 LEFT Everyone, from La Fontaine to Robespierre to Diderot, let themselves be tempted by the excellence of the café Procope. Local lore even claims that a newly appointed young lieutenant, one Napoleon Bonaparte, once had to pay for his coffee at the Procope by pledging his hat as security.

212 CENTER AND RIGHT The Brasserie Lipp opened in 1880 (center); its regulars (Proust and Camus, for example, but also an impressive series of future politicians and actors) were so significant the government included it in the list of "Memorable Places." The Grand Véfour (right) has been part of the history of Paris since the eighteenth century: there's Colette's favorite table, there's Napoleon's, Hugo's . . .

213 LEFT The golden days of the Belle Epoque carry on in the Grand Salon at Maxim's. The legendary Parisian restaurant was opened in 1893 by a former waiter, Maxime Gaillard, who removed the last vowel from his first name in homage to the anglophile fashion of the time.

213 RIGHT The head sommelier at Tour d'Argent ponders a bottle that is bound to be extremely valuable: this restaurant, famous for its view of the Seine, is considered the quintessence of luxury, even in Paris.

214-215, 216 AND 217 The staff at Maxim's, from the concierge at the entrance to the waiters, is comprised of high-class professionals. The wine stewards, for example, can "customize" what they serve, depending on the client's appearance and behavior; similarly, the flower arranger is a famous artist and the head waiter is also a cigar expert.

Speaking of François Rabelais, he was an eminently Parisian author who gave French literature one of its most truculent characters—Pantagruel. This gigantic glutton who baked everything that contributed to rounding out his stomach did not, alas, have the opportunity to dine in a restaurant, because in his time, the fifteenth century, restaurants did not yet exist.

Of course, there were inns along the roads and taverns in the cities, but you ate what you found, when you found something. The word "restaurant" appeared in the eighteenth century and suggested a horrible meat broth that was meant to "restore" the hungry person or put him back on his feet.

Restaurants as we know them came about at the time of the Revolution, when the sansculottes created unemployment for the cooks of the aristocrats whose heads they had chopped off, inducing the chefs to make more democratic use of their talents. The first restaurant to be set up in Paris was the Grand Véfour, which still exists. It was such a success that in three years, the owner made a fortune and, fearing the jealousy and arbitrary accusations of his less fortunate colleagues, went elsewhere to see if the leeks were greener. Anthelme Brillat-Savarin, the first of a long list of Parisian culinary critics, wrote his highly celebrated essay, "The Physiology of Taste," which, in the preface, has this definitive sentence: "Animals fill their stomachs; men feed themselves; only people of wit have the enjoyment of eating."

That's why soon people of wit, flagellated by their egos, frequented the place that welcomed Lamartine, Saint-Beuve, and Victor Hugo, for whom the cook prepared breast of mutton with white beans, which the writer was crazy about.

Another must-see place for lovers of terrestrial and spiritual food is Le Procope. The story of this tavern is anything but trite.

Opened by a sharp-witted Italian, Procopio Dei Coltelli

introduced coffee to France. In 1689, he had the stroke of good luck to see the Comédie Française install itself opposite. Procope became the waiting room—and sometimes the room—of the first theater in France, where authors and actors made dates with the loose women of the time. For a long time, the Procope contented itself with its standing as a café/ice cream parlor before becoming, with the Revolution, the restaurant of Danton, Marat, and Robespierre. The Procope contributed to the Parisians' imagination—it saw Denis Diderot at work on his *Encyclopédie,* Verlaine bent over his glass of absinthe, and the elegant Oscar Wilde rapping on the table with his cane to call the waiter.

Certainly, until the end of the nineteenth century, men of wit did not go to restaurants with their wives. These places had bad reputations and decency prevents evoking here what the women of good society imagined could happen on the velvet sofas hidden by brocade curtains.

It seems, although it remains unproven, that the scratches on the mirrors of Lapérouse and Maxim's were left by the "horizontal ones"— loose women whose profession we can guess from the image suggested by the word—who, in this way, tested the authenticity of the diamonds offered to them by their very wealthy lovers.

Paris is proud of its old restaurants, which it calls "literary." They are the scenes of the social theater of the capital where one goes to eat but also—and most important—to see and be seen. There are at least fifteen that you cannot do without, where you meet the Paris that counts and the curi-

ous who come with the hope of encountering a glorious superstar.

To count the restaurants that, in Paris, voluntarily show off the list of the personalities of every type who frequent them would be a prodigious task. They are all those restaurants in which words are said, in a relaxing moment, that inspire books, articles, replicas of actors, or poems that leave a lasting impression in time.

They include the Brasserie Lipp at the Dôme; the Coupole al Boeuf sur le Toit, created by Jean Cocteau; and Lucas-Carton and Maxim's, both owned by the designer Pierre Cardin. Maxim's is a Paris legend. This restaurant from the Belle Époque was the setting for the follies of a decadent society that opened champagne with a saber and played Russian roulette for its life. Princes in exile, bankers, ministers, film stars, poets, musicians, divas, and high-ranking coquettes have fixed in the collective unconscious the image of a Paris carefree, refined, worldly, and disenchanted to the point of suicide.

The other sanctuary of Parisian good taste is the Tour d'Argent, which has a unique view on the Seine that has made millions of Americans dream. Absolute luxury. One of the most important points of reference in international gastronomy, it is also inserted into the programs of foreign kings and presidents on their official visits to the capital. But to have one of the four most desirable tables in the world, those that are by the windows overhanging the Seine, you have to book a couple of years ahead.

218 AND 218-219 The brasserie La Coupole, on Boulevard de Montparnasse, was opened in 1927 in what used to be a wood and coal depot. Since then, a lot of water has passed under the bridges of Paris: over time, this establishment has become the meeting place for everyone who counts in the art world of the Rive Gauche.

220-221 Subtle shadows pass through the ground floor hall of the Hôtel Ambassador, which boasts beautiful pink marble columns. Another illustrious name, this luxury hotel regained its look of the past thanks to careful renovation work.

222-223 The Buddha Bar welcomes its clientele in an atmosphere that is more heterogeneous than Asian, despite the statue that towers over the room.

223 Another ultra-cool bar is Man Ray, which is "twinned" with one of the same name in New York, and is therefore at the height of fashion. Here, too, the atmosphere is meant to be that of the Far East, so at the bar, you can sit on the floor.

224 The empire of the great restaurants and the small, pleasant world of cafés and bistros are closer than they seem, because the common denominator is always that indefinable Parisian charm. So, broadly speaking, haute cuisine and a quick *repas* end up tasting the same.

225 Round tables that can barely hold a coffee cup, the all-important ashtray, and the smell of dark tobacco in the air: the dreamlike atmosphere of some bistros—in this case, in the eighteenth arrondissement, not far from the underground station of Anvers—naturally maintains a feel of the dearly remembered realist cinema.

That said, even if you do not find a place in one of these famous restaurants, you do not risk dying of hunger in Paris. The telephone book has a list of 2,500 restaurants, and ten new ones open every week. In this melting pot, each gourmand finds something that suits him, depending on his culinary tastes and the thickness of his wallet. Among the Vietnamese, African, Spanish, Italian, Moroccan, Lebanese, and other restaurants, there is a long list of foreign chefs who attempt to seduce the Parisians with their more or less folkloric specialties. Recently, the fashion was cafés furnished in the high-tech style dear to New Yorkers, where the portions and the clientele are both in the same style—minimalist. Cafés *à la mode* last from three weeks to three months with, in the old style, the specials of the day written in chalk on large blackboards.

But there's a thorn planted in the heart of every Parisian gifted with a palate. Paris, which poses as the universal capital of gastronomy, has unfortunately joined the trend for fast food and self-service. Fortunately, however, there still are places that continue the tradition of table as opposed to bar service.

These are the aces of great cuisine, celebrated by culinary critics who award their stars, arrows, chefs hats, and other symbols in which Parisians blindly believe. Evidently the numbers and the quality of recognition increase the final bill, sometimes to a dizzying amount. But who, at least once in his life, doesn't dream of dining at Pierre Gagnaire's, Alain Passard's, Guy Savoy's, or Alain Ducasse's? The cuisine of the great chefs has something ingenious, even miraculous. And so it is normal that Ledoyen, l'Arpège, Plaza Athénée, Jules Verne, and others, with their pres-

tigious names and starched tablecloths, define the gastronomic itinerary of Paris.

Paris is also famous for its bistros. It is there that the people, those Parisians of more modest means, come during their lunch breaks to hurriedly eat their beefsteak and fried potatoes, washing them down with a glass of red wine followed by a good cup of coffee. Real bistros are disappearing, giving their places to wine stores and sex shops. Real bistros were eateries where the owner knew everyone and acted as the newspaper of the quarter, and where his wife knew when to give credit. They were called "At Susette's" or "Friends' Meeting Place." Two umbrellas on the sidewalk. Four crooked wooden tables where lovers carved their names in a heart. Checkered tablecloths. Large jars of mustard. The owner's wife at the stove; the owner at the counter. The card game in the back of the room. The radio tuned to the race results. The Homeric arguments about the Tour de France, which always ended with volleys of racy jokes in front of a glass of Picon-bière. In the evening, the young boys met around a pinball machine, beating time with their feet to the yé-yé songs, gum in their mouths, to impress the girl on the sixth floor, whom they often met on the stairs but never approached.

Francis Carco, Léon-Paul Fargue, Antoine Blondin—the sites of your old bistros have already entered into Montmartre's museum. And if from where you are, you don't take action, the cementers of space, the slaughterers of a kind, will soon have finished with that Paris that you loved so much. The Paris that survives only in childhood memories, the stories of our grandparents, and the albums of yellowed photographs.

226-227 "Here water is used for boiling potatoes": this sign hangs on a beam on the ceiling. That phrase perfectly sums up the spirit of the bistros in the best tradition, where wine is almost a pretext for meeting, talking, and tasting genuine food and drink.

228-229 Everyone knows that "the way things were" is always better than how they are today: a happy application of this nostalgic conservatism is evident in the unbeatable Parisian bistros and *relais*, where precious art déco mosaics provide the setting for the menus in the windows.

230 Chalked menus of the day and sweeping on the Montmartre pavements. Paris obviously has numerous Internet cafés and high-tech bars, but when fashion and technology pass, it is the old-time bistros that remain, unchanged and loved by all.

231 Before opening, a zealous owner cleans the awning on the bar's terrace, which is completely invaded by a screen of chairs that are piled up according to a time-honored system.

232 AND 233 Saint Germain des Prés, Montmartre, and Marais: three quarters in the heart of Paris are represented in these images of *salons de thé* in ultra-traditional style. What they have in common is history, from the Jacobin revolution to the decapitation, in the third century, of St. Denis Bishop of Lutetia on the Mons Martyrium, up to the people's destruction of the Bastille in the Marais.

234-235 Early in the morning, a *crêperie-friterie* opens up to whet the appetite of the day's clients. French fries and crêpes are the most popular items on the hurried menus of passers-by—the Parisians out of habit and the non-Parisians by happy discovery.

236 AND 237 The Parisian idea of the *PLAT À EMPORTER* (a turn of phrase that, thanks to the undisputed elegance of the French language, sounds less brutal than "takeout") does not even contemplate precooked foods, as demonstrated by the wines, quiches, croissants, and *PAINS AU CHOCOLAT* in these windows on the Ile Saint Louis.

238-239 The "empire style" composure of the products and decor does not deceive the connoisseur: Paris is no less famous than Vienna for its exquisite pastry making.

239 RIGHT The generic neon-lit shops that nowadays invade the center of any big city have no place in the nostalgic geography of the Paris of the palate: as is shown by this artistic decoration at the entrance to an *ÉPICERIE*, the shopkeepers care about the appearance of their shops no less than about the goodness of their wares.

SPECIALITE
DE
TARTES CHAUDES
SALEES
A TOUTE HEURE
Anniversaire
1944
1994

240 THE ARTISTIC CHAOS ON THE DRAWING TABLE IN THE EMBROIDERY ATELIER OF LESAGE ANNOUNCES THE UNIVERSE OF CREATION: HUNDREDS OF HOURS OF WORK WILL BE NECESSARY TO SATISFY CLIENTS SUCH AS YVES SAINT-LAURENT.

241 LEFT AND RIGHT TODAY, NAMES SUCH AS COCO CHANEL AND NINA RICCI ARE EVOCATIVE OF LUXURY, BEAUTY, ELEGANCE: THESE TWO TOP COUTURIERES HAVE COME A LONG WAY FROM THE EARLY DAYS WHEN THEY THOUGHT UP THEIR FIRST DESIGNS. IT WAS IN THE IMPOVERISHED YEARS AFTER WORLD WAR II THAT BOTH BEGAN TO WORK WITH SALVAGED MATERIALS.

PARIS
OF LUXURY

Paris did not invent the word "luxury," which comes from Latin, but over the centuries, it gave it the credentials of nobility.

Luxury is what you feel when you have a unique object, made only for you, belonging only to you—a sign of your uniqueness, your originality compared to others.

It is, to some degree, a custom-made dream.

Paris, the most dreamy city in the galaxy, has logically established itself as the capital of luxury. To evoke the luxury of Paris, you would need a dissertation similar to a beautiful dress on a beautiful woman, both long enough to cover the subject and short enough to attract attention.

You would also need to add to it the price that this unique dress justifies. But already here you distance yourself from luxury by falling into commerce, one of the most vulgar notions that refers to vain exhibitionists and other *nouveaux riches*, who show off designer names so that they become only labels meant to attest to their social standing. But luxury is never ostentatious. The objects and attitudes that distinguish luxury are the indispensable complements of elegance. They are the characteristics of a certain art of living. They are discreet. People of luxury are like all other people but they are not just any people; they know that money isn't what counts but rather the way in which you spend it.

Paris knows this, too, since often in the course of its history it has paid dearly for its freedom with gold that it did not always have.

Luxury involves a world of initiates who don't need advertising to know that the saddles made in the Hermès atelier have no equals; that a vine stock of Château Yquem produces only one glass of wine every two years; that the embroidery on Saint-Laurent's evening gowns done by Lesage required hundreds of hours of work, without any possibility of error; and that, at Lalique, generations of master glassblowers have patiently learned to dominate the rough material to make of it an absolutely perfect glass.

The luxury of Paris is defined by a series of famous patronymics that are the proud designer names of the rue de la Paix, Faubourg Saint Honoré, Avenue Montaigne, and Place Vendôme. This itinerary is specifically Parisian, demarcated by the golden triangle (Avenue Montaigne, Champs Elysées, Georges V, and the streets within) and the Comité Colbert square (rue du Faubourg Saint Honoré, Franklin Roosevelt, Matignon, la Boëtie, and the streets nearby). Two quarters, which among other images, transmit impressions of chic and elegance. These are addresses not to be missed in the "art of living" in the French style, an intimate mixture of culture, passion for beauty and quality, and a sense of innovation and creativity. It is the French taste par excellence. The Parisians simply call it taste.

Luxury objects can be cataloged. They are found in all settings. The arts of the table, leather goods, trips in private airplanes or in first class, wines of which only one or two bottles remain, diamonds as big as the Ritz, books in limited, numbered editions, Van Gogh's *Sunflowers* above the fireplace, and giving yourself the right to come to Paris in April even if only to see the lilacs flowering behind Notre Dame.

243 LUXURY" AND "ELEGANCE," NOT TO MENTION "HIGH FASHION," SEEM TO ENJOY A SPECIAL STATUS IN PARIS—A SPECIAL STATUS OF AUTONOMY AND MORAL JUSTIFICATION. THE SLIGHTLY SURREAL ATMOSPHERE AT THE FASHION SHOWS, FOR EXAMPLE, DOES NOT SUIT ANY OTHER CITY IN QUITE THE SAME WAY, NO MATTER HOW MODERN OR ACTIVE IT IS. ESSENTIALLY, IN THIS "CITY FOR DREAMING," THE EPHEMERAL AND THE SUPERFLUOUS APPEAR MORE NATURAL AND EVEN MORE USEFUL THAN ELSEWHERE, AS IS DEMONSTRATED BY THE UNCONDITIONAL, GLOBAL SUCCESS OF THE GREAT FASHION LABELS THAT WERE BORN HERE.

Haute couture, however, dominates the entire image of luxury.

In this case, though, it was Paris that invented the words in 1947, when the young lions of the needle and scissors set up an organization more dynamic than that created by their predecessors. The couturiers, the tailors, were defined as "great" because their imagination, their sense of invention and research, their ability to constantly renew a vision of clothing according to changes in society, and their capacity to adapt to the essence of the times made them artistic creators. Thus, they distinguished themselves from ready-made clothing manufacturers, from classical tailors, and from seamstresses offering custom-made clothes. They wrapped their dresses, coats, skirts, and blouses not only in monogrammed silk paper but also in an almost cultural discourse that exalted the spirit of the times, the originality and exclusivity of the models and the fabric as well as the fact that each piece, being unique, was a work of art in itself.

Paul Poiret, who dressed the Belle Époque and the Années Folles, launched the movement, followed, between the wars, by Lucien Lelong, Maggy Rouff, and Madeleine Vionnet.

The period after World War II was an uncertain time that did not invite luxury. It was a time of drastic recessions, which especially hit the textile industry, already in a bad state from the war. Parisians had more to worry about than following fashion. As for the tailors, they were competing in ingenuity to economize on that small amount of fabric that they found. Without the basic materials, they made clothes that adhered to the body as much as possible, with three-quarter sleeves set into the highest part of the shoulder and skirts as short as decency permitted. It should be remembered that, in that period, Jacques Fath cut his suits from American army blankets and Jean Dessès made his evening gowns from parachutes.

Elsa Schiapparelli used the zipper (invented by Hermès to replace buttons). Salvatore Ferragamo put hinged wooden soles on his boiled leather galoshes. Nina Ricci used fabrics from the Occupation made with a vegetable base—the ancestor of our viscose—that the Parisians believed bloomed in the first days of spring, and Jeanne Lanvin signed the linings of her clothes because brand-name fabric makers had completely disappeared. As for Coco Chanel, who had taken refuge in Switzerland, she made her first famous suit in 1953 with scraps of fabric sewn together with very small stitches and accessorized it with long necklaces made of chains of brass thread bought by the meter from a bankrupt lighting manufacturer. It was the prototype of a style later copied by millions of women. Chanel was very much accustomed to coping. Immediately after World War I, she had the idea for her famous dark blue suspender dresses after discovering a stock of tubular (seamless) jersey, which was intended for the manufacture of underwear for soldiers. She invented "poor chic."

Christian Dior, on the other hand, spectacularly solidified the concept of luxury in fashion. In 1947, rejecting the austerity, monotony, and pessimism of the time, this young designer, who was also shy, dictated his vision of elegance without taking any pecuniary considerations into account. He allied himself with Marcel Boussac, a textile manufacturer, who wove for him cashmere yarn imported from Ireland and imported silk and brocades from India and furs from Canada.

The first Christian Dior collection was like a bolt from the blue. Skirts to the ankle inflated like balloons, supported by layers of underskirts of silk-lined horsehair, enlarged armholes, shoulder pads, dresses fitted at the waist, shawl coats so large as to slip from the shoulders at the slightest movement. Everything was done in sumptuous and iridescent fabric, cut and sewn by hand and embroidered with motifs and precious stones, work of extreme precision that had required months of patience for the workers of the atelier reopened for the occasion. Abundance was at its height. This collection led to the famous remark by Carmel Snow, the fashion editor of *Vogue* magazine: "It's definitely a new look!"

244 "PALACE" IS THE TERM USED TO DESIGNATE THE BEST PARISIAN HOTELS. IN SHORT, THEY ARE SOMETHING MORE THAN JUST HOTELS: ALL VERY FAMOUS NAMES, ALMOST HOTELS PAR EXCELLENCE, THE PALACES ARE ABOVE ALL PLACES IN WHICH HISTORY, AND LEGEND, HAS BEEN MADE.

246 AND 247 THERE IS NO DENYING THAT THE WORLD OF LUXURY SPEAKS FRENCH, OR RATHER EXPRESSES ITSELF IN A VERY PARISIAN ARGOT. FROM THE MOST VALUABLE, HIGH QUALITY AND YEARNED-AFTER JEWELERY IN THE WORLD TO STYLISH SADDLES FOR THOROUGHBREDS, THE GOODS OF THE *JOAILLIERS* SUCH AS CARTIER AND THE *PELLETIERS* LIKE HERMÈS FILL THE ENTRIES IN THE DICTIONARY OF ELEGANCE.

So luxury is not fashion. It is even the opposite of fashion. Fashion is what one does. Luxury, instead, plays on the entire range of contradictions with the first thing that happens, the everyday, the agreed upon, the new idea thrown out that soon ends up in the wardrobe. Fashion is the things that one buys. Luxury is what one chooses with a single criterion of desire or emotion. Fashion is transitory. Luxury is eternal and speaks of the exceptional. For this reason, in luxury, everything is great.

Great designers, great hairdressers, great shoemakers, great restaurants . . . not content to mark its difference in a mundane way, luxury took refuge behind a vocabulary that has also been able to export its text in French. So in New York, Tokyo, Madrid, London, or Rome, everyone knows that Louis Vuitton is not a handbag and luggage manufacturer but rather a *malletier*; that Cartier is not a jeweler but rather a *joaillier*; that at Porthaud, they do not sell sheets and pillowcases but rather *linge de lit*; that at Hermès, there are no scarves but rather *carré*; that Roger Vivier is not a shoe manufacturer but rather a *bottier*; that at Berluti, they do not make men's shoes, but rather they are *souliers*; and that l'Arpege is not a great restaurant, but rather a *grande table*.

As for the Crillon and the Ritz, they are not hotels but palaces.

This is truly the real picture of luxury. There are half a dozen Paris hotels that merit the word *palace,* luxurious hotel, because to go through their doors means entering effortlessly into the dream and the legend. The *palaces* in Paris are unique of their kind for one reason at least: they are all protected landmarks and are located in exceptional places. The Meurice is right in front of the Tuileries gardens, and the balcony of the famous Suite 702-4 surveys all of Paris. It overlooks at once the pyramid of the Louvre, Notre Dame, les Invalides, and the Pantheon. Imagine the spectacle when Paris turns on its lights. The Crillon hotel on the Place de la Concorde, originally a private residence built by Count Crillon, a descendent of a comrade-in-arms of Henry IV, was opened in 1788. The Bristol was built right in the heart of the legendary and luxurious Faubourg Saint Honoré. The George V, opened in 1928, right in the middle of the Roaring Twenties, is a large vessel landed between the Champs Elysées and the Eiffel Tower, right in the center of the golden triangle, on the most aristocratic thoroughfare in Paris. The Royal Monceau is a former convent, converted into a hotel in 1924, in Avenue Hoche, one of the two or three most prestigious addresses in the capital. The Plaza Athénée, opened in 1911, is found on the famous Avenue Montaigne, sanctuary of fashion, spectacle, and business. The Ritz, perhaps the most legendary place in Paris, inspired one of F. Scott Fitzgerald's best stories, "The Diamond As Big As the Ritz." It is located in Place Vendôme, near the gold and diamonds of the most celebrated *joailliers* in the world.

The luxurious Parisian hotels also have in common the fact that they are protected places where time and space have no power. When you enter them, you immediately perceive that the gilded ceilings, the mirrors, the marble, and the wooden paneling are mute witnesses to the history of Paris. Here treaties have been signed, nations have been born, new borders have been traced on the map of the General Staff, peace agreements have been discussed, and armistices negotiated. Here the lives and destinies of millions of individuals have been decided.

The Parisian *palaces* are coffers. The history of Paris happens in these places and goes back in time to the follies of the Belle Époque,

248-249 The ubiquity of references to luxury shouldn't come as a shock in Paris, especially along the Champs Elysées or in fashion havens such as rue Montaigne.

250-251 Hands guided by the necessity for unerring good taste and for an excellent, flawless product are at work in the Lesage embroidery workshops (left) and in the Chanel atelier (right), in preparation for the next fashion shows.

FROM 252 TO 255 *Printemps, été, automne, hiver.* Parisian seasons are defined not only by the whims of the weather but also by those of haute couture.

to the court of Louis XV, to the aristocratic tables of the eighteenth century. Luxury here is wedded to the definitive present.

The armchairs in the Bristol lobby, purchased from the Louvre before World War II, belonged to Queen Marie Antoinette. The tapestry that decorates the Galerie de la Paix in the George V is from the seventeenth century, and the fireplace in the Louis XII salon is from the Renaissance. The presidential suites in the Crillon are furnished in pure Louis XV and Louis XVI, and the Braques and Miròs on the walls are authentic. The ceilings of the restaurant of the Hôtel Meurice were painted by Poilpot, and the mosaics on the floor were walked upon by the Sultan of Zanzibar, Napoleon III, Paul Poiret, Prince Aga Khan, General de Gaulle, Winston Churchill, the Grand Duchess of Russia, and the Maharajah of Japur.

The legend of Paris's *palaces* also involves the celebrities who visit them. Cohorts of stars, politicians, kings, and presidents, financial and business magnates, top models, jet-set personalities—a whole world of luxury. You have the feeling that occupying their beds and their bathrooms, you become a little more intimate with them. Intimate with Madonna, who, in one of her videos, runs naked on the blue and pink carpets of the second floor of the Royal Monceau. How could you forget that Suites 101 and 158 were occupied by Theodore Roosevelt, King George V of England, Emperor Hirohito, and John Fitzgerald and Jacqueline Kennedy, and that here General Eisenhower made an appointment with Marshal Montgomery to celebrate the Liberation of Paris? Montgomery left in his room the American flag that he had waved during the first part of the disembarkation; it was later returned to the United States. Here, again in 1947, Ho Chi Minh was a guest, invited to the Fontainebleau Conference while France and Vietnam were still at war. How would it be possible for the salons of the first floor of the Crillon not to evoke the birth of the League of Nations, which would become the United Nations, the first meeting of which was held here? And how could you not bring relativity to the misunderstandings that the American and French people are now having when you know that, on February 6, 1778, when this place was not yet a hotel, Benjamin Franklin signed the Franco-American treaty in which France recognized the United States's act of independence? How could you not evoke the silhouettes of Fitzgerald and Hemingway sitting side by side at the bar of the Ritz and not imagine that, if a machine existed that could take you back in time, you could think of having tea with Musidora, Jean Cocteau, Audrey Hepburn, and Marlene Dietrich in the suite that Coco Chanel occupied all year round and in which she left her precious Coromandel lacquer screens?

Life in the Parisian palaces is also the stuff of legend. At the Crillon, in a basement reserved for that purpose, are stored the personal effects of certain clients who return regularly and want to find the furniture, objects, books, and clothing in their rooms exactly in the same place as they left them when they were last there. At the Royal Monceau, they remember that rock star who, exactly at midnight, requested a live python for a photographic session. It took only an hour for the doorman to deliver the reptile loaned from a circus in the capital. At the Ritz, they still speak of that client on a business trip who asked to have four thousand roses sent to his young wife who had remained in Cairo. And it was done within a day.

Paris is the uncontested epicenter of luxury. It is proud of this and lays claim to it.

Voltaire knew this very well. He mockingly said that the Parisians could forgive everything as long as they were recognized as having the best tailors, custom shoemakers, hairdressers, perfume shops, jewelry stores, leather goods shops, cooks, and hotels in the world.

The luxury of Paris: close-up of the gleam of a pearl, the flash of a diamond in the neckline of a tweed suit. Front shot of a long black limousine that slowly glides onto the wet roadway of the Place Vendôme and a Ritz bellboy, umbrella in hand, taking two tawny leather suitcases from the trunk of a Jaguar E. At the bar of the Lutecia, close-up of a glass of port, a Cuban cigar smoldering in a crystal ashtray, a man's hand given prominence by a shirt cuff fastened by a gold button with his initials.

But in Paris, the luxury of luxuries is time, that which belongs to people who are not in a hurry. Their compensation is to see what others never see, to be witnesses to the romance of Paris, this endless *feuilleton*, or serial, consisting of moments of tenderness, nonevents, and anonymous gestures, which lay the foundations of history.

Paris is the capital of luxury—all luxuries, even that of sowing your own dreams to harvest memories.

CITY OF LIGHT AND SHADOWS

LA VILLE
LUMIÈRE

You might think that Paris sleeps at night. But it doesn't. As soon as dusk falls, Paris lights up. Paris awakens. The magic of light: Paris redesigns its silhouette, puts on its makeup, and becomes a mosaic of clashing shades. There are 365 bulbs in the lamps of the Place de la Concorde, to set the style. Then there are the Trocadero fountains that gurgle in streams of light and the monuments that light up, one after the other. Notre Dame leaves its ordinary daily existence behind to enter into eternity and perhaps beyond. When there is fog, the Tour Saint Jacques seems to feel the cold, wrapping a boa of swan feathers around its shoulders. On the façades of the Louvre, the Conciergerie, and the Invalides, ghosts are created from the play of light and shadow. The Eiffel Tower flickers like a turn indicator and, from a distance, looks like a bottle of champagne or a Lido dancer. The bridges, too, come to life, spectacularly connecting one bank to the other. To be seen, they emphasize themselves with yellow, sprinkling gold below. They mask themselves like witches and throw off cabalistic signs that indicate adventurous direction to the eyes of the late-night wanderer. Pont Alexandre III and its statues, candelabras, garlands of iron, all that baroque decoration that the artificial light puts into relief

much more at night than during the day. Passerelle des Arts, a wooden bridge so fragile that you fear to set foot on it. Pont Neuf, that Christo wrapped with a *plissé* of angel's wings which, covering the parapets, the roadbed, and even the lamps, give it a ghostly bearing. The Champs Elysées, seen from above from the Arc de Triomphe, is a long red serpent of cars that descends toward la Concorde and a long white serpent of cars that ascends toward l'Etoile, the green, yellow, and red lights like the lighted buoys of ships. On the Seine, there is a long procession of *bateaux-mouches*. Here you dine through two thousand years of history. Façades of monuments and houses, in passing blinded by floodlights set in the gunwales. Sparks of light on the statues of the Museum of Modern Art, which seem decorated for a nocturnal cult. Offshore towers lit from within crisscross like immense photophores. The Montparnasse tower, with its rectangular windows randomly illuminated by the office lamps that hurried accountants have forgotten to turn off, resembles an immense painting by Piet Mondrian. Between two bands of light that sweep the riverbank, you glimpse furtive movements under the bridges. Criminals, vagrants, or lovers—who knows? Night in Paris is a land of illusions.

261 A perfect sentimental parameter for measuring any phenomenon that has to do with light, the nighttime panorama of the Ville Lumière is enriched by magnificent fireworks on July 14, the anniversary of the storming of the Bastille.

Fireworks over Paris. On the flat roofs of the solid bourgeois dwellings on rue Raynouard moves a crowd of Chinese shadows. Tuxedos. Evening dress. Some armchairs have been lifted up. Valets in white gloves circulate with unstable balance on the pebbles, carrying silver trays loaded with petits-fours and flutes of champagne. The colors fall like rain, filling the sky and fading into the Seine. All this is the "ordinary" spectacle of Paris by night, that which it offers for free when it escapes from the contingencies and natural laws of the day and transforms itself into a magic kaleidoscope, repeated into the infinity of future nights. A wise Paris. Civilized. Exclusively effervescent in the places agreed upon or allowed.

But, for some, nights in Paris willingly coincide with the extraordinary and the intense. In these cases, it is the Paris that remains in the heart like a sting and in the head like an illumination, and sometimes like a regret that the adventure did not go beyond the game of parallel lives.

Nights are not the same on Grand Boulevard, Pigalle, and the Champs Elysées.

Parisian nights do not come with instructions. There's every chance of reconstituting the city according to your own needs and wandering around in search of what you wish to find. The field of possibilities varies according to the individual and to the real, supposed, and expected delights. At night, in Paris, the limits that separate the reasonable from what is less so are totally outside of time and escape moral or social classifications.

What can you put into a night in Paris? Everything—dreams, phantoms, pleasures, and the sum of your own wishes. You can even put limits on your own freedom of being.

Paris by night is a city of sects, tribes, networks. It's based on rituals, linguistic codes, dress conventions. *Danseurs-visages,* people who go beyond the limits. Here, each one, in relation to his or her personal story, finds a piece of the city that fits.

Saint Germain, neon bleeding on the pavement, the Deux Magots and Flore where existentialism has degrees, has regrets. New Wave was shipwrecked in the gutters of rue des Canettes, the Buci crossroads, rue Saint Benoît. From Lipp, the curls of cigar smoke sting the eyes of the young girls perching on stools, who cross their often beautiful legs high up, their gaze full of golden spangles.

Les Halles quarter. Jazz clubs from which come the wailing of a trumpet, the staccato of a drum. The streets fill with black and white butterflies like the keys of a piano. Where you pay your weight in gold to sit on the terrace of a café.

262 AND 263 AMONG THE MANY RECORDS IT HOLDS, PARIS BOASTS THAT OF THE MOST FAMOUS AND WIDELY IMITATED MUSIC HALLS. THE MOULIN ROUGE, (LEFT, THE FAMOUS SIGN), THEATRE DES FOLIES BERGÈRE (RIGHT, DURING A CANCAN SHOW), AND LIDO, WHOSE SIGN STANDS OUT IN THE NIGHT ON AVENUE DES CHAMPS ELYSÉES, ARE NAMES THAT HAVE BECOME MODERN MYTHS OF NIGHTLIFE.

264-265 A *BATEAU–MOUCHE,* A TERM THAT'S IN THE EMOTIONAL VOCABULARY OF ROMANTICS ALL OVER THE WORLD, GLIDES TOWARD THE ILE DE LA CITÉ AND NOTRE DAME DE PARIS. AT LEFT, PONT AU DOUBLE SHOWS THE WAY TO THE LATIN QUARTER.

Champs Elysées. Large cabarets with bare-breasted dancers. Crazy Horse and Lido. Dancers adorned with so many plumes that no ostrich would be able to support their weight.

Place du Tertre. Smoky cafés, boutiques selling souvenir T-shirts. Painters who forever offer a thousand variations on a single theme—that of an ingenuous, ideal, prettified Paris—that end up on the walls of living rooms in Philadelphia, Sydney, or Singapore. Further down, there's Place Blanche, Pigalle, Barbès. Dismal cabarets. Artificial paradises. A choice of eroticism. After Marthe Richard, who closed up the brothels, only the image seduces, depending on the advertising posters placed at the entrance of taverns and hotels of ill repute.

Parc Monceau. Private gambling salons, discreet places, secrets known by rare initiates.

Clubs, discotheques, nocturnal bars throw down their anchors in improbable places, somewhat attacked by the Paris that crowds them and then abandons them without apparent reason. The fashion in our times is for new bars, often created by showbiz stars. These are the chic, discreet, toned-down places where you find the Paris that counts. The Buddha Bar, the Café Coste, the Man Ray, the Nirvana, whose musical compilations sell like hotcakes and are exported throughout the world.

But the nocturnal élite can be recognized by the fact that it flees the common and abandons a particular sanctuary because the intensive presence of other people diminishes its symbolic value.

Belleville, Ménilmontant, rue de Lappe, and Canal Saint Martin are the new centers of nocturnal pleasures. You dance the tango, the latest craze of Parisian nights, at the Trottoirs d'Argentina and the salsa at the Latina Bar Club. You clap your hands and stamp your feet, standing on the tables, to accompany the flamenco dancers at the Spanish Harlem club.

In Paris, there are Brazilian nights of batucada drums, which plunge into the esoteric inferno of the macumba of African nights measured by the voodoo tamtams of the Chappelle. Arab nights, Chinese nights, Russian nights . . . an infinity of nights in Paris that sink their roots into the cultures of all times, of all countries. There are also dazzling nights that illegally occupy unused warehouses or abandoned factories. Wild nights in which you move forward masked by dark glasses amid the screeching of electronic music.

Paris is a tireless and feverish city.

In the morning, the pigeons lift themselves in flight from the chignons of the statues where they have made their nests and the garbage collectors push the dreams and trash into the gutter.

This evening will be another night in Paris.

266-267 The lights of sunset flicker for a last instant on the blue patina of time: the cherubs on the base of a streetlight on Pont Alexandre III get ready to cross the Parisian night.

268-269 Pillars of light emerge in the firmament of the Ville Lumière: the Hôtel de Ville, bristling with chimneys, and Notre Dame rise above an invisible Seine, which is hidden by the buildings on Ile de la Cité and the surrounding areas.

270-271 The Pyramide by I. M. Pei, a timeless symbol of the eternity that the Louvre has regained, is the tip of an iceberg: underground, the structure encloses the basements of the Cour Napoleon and the Cour du Carrousel.

272-273 The Arc de Triomphe is the glorious fulcrum for Place de l'Etoile, the convergence of avenues dedicated to great soldiers like Foch and Marceau. This enormous intersection has seen the parades of armies of invaders and liberators, which have now been replaced by streams of traffic going in and out of the center of Paris.

274-275 Through the enormous line of Champ-de-Mars, the four-footed base of the Eiffel Tower encloses the entire building of the Ecole Militaire in a vast bubble.

276 The Eiffel Tower has as many different looks as it has views and potential light conditions. Everyone has their favorite, but at night, this cascade of liquid gold seems almost excessive in its splendor.

277 Under the burst of floodlights, an entire cosmos of intricate geometries explodes toward the observer who stands at the foot of the Eiffel Tower, almost exactly at the center of the base.

278 Today, as in the late nineteenth century, the Grand Foyer of the Opéra Garnier enfolds Parisian high society in the rococo glory of the Grand Escalier.

278-279 With its rich arrangement of solids, the eclectically opulent façade of the Opéra—very *deuxième empire*—adorns the square named for the opera.

280 and 280-281 The international shrine of music, the Opéra Garnier is also an important venue for ballet. Spectators who hope to meet the ballet artists between acts or want to see them rehearse their steps flock to the Foyer de la Danse, in the back of the building.

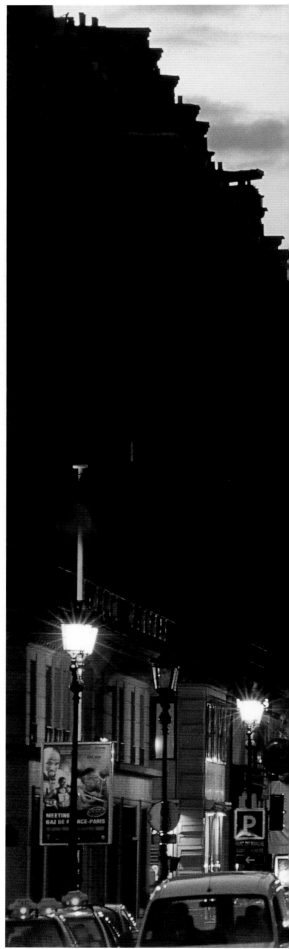

282-283 From a good vantage point such as the Eiffel Tower, the esplanade of Champ-de-Mars is visible to its full extent, up to the brightly lit Ecole Militaire. At left, the fabric of the city has a prominent point in the dome of the Hôtel des Invalides.

284-285 In the heart of Paris at night, the tenuous threads of a cobweb of lights are concentrated at the corners of a perfect radiant triangle: the Eiffel Tower, the Dome des Invalides, and the Arc de Triomphe.

FROM 286 TO 289 The names of Valentin le Désossé and Jean Avril are distant memories, but the myth of the Moulin Rouge comes to life every evening on Boulevard de Clichy, at the southern edge of Montmartre.

290 AND 291 Wearing cobalt ostrich feathers and dazzling sequins, the Bluebell Girls of the Lido bring a Las Vegas atmosphere to Parisian nights.

292 AND 293 The Pink Grand Finale of the show at the Moulin Rouge is a noisy, "very Parisian" cancan led by the athletic dancer Igor: although it uses the most modern show business techniques, every night the Moulin Rouge re-creates the dream of an era that would otherwise have disappeared.

294 AND 295 The signs of the Moulin Rouge are of highly respectable, almost archetypal descent: indeed, in 1889 it was this legendary nightclub that launched the era of the illuminated advertising sign.

INDEX

PHOTO CREDITS

300   Facing west, in the direction of North America, mirroring its "older sister" who guards the entrance to New York Harbor, a copy of the Statue of Liberty lighting up the world stands on the Ile des Cygnes on the Seine. The monument was given to France by the United States on the occasion of the Universal Exposition in 1889, three years after the gift of the original was made. Originally, however, the monument faced east, toward the Elysée.

Thunder Bay Press
An imprint of the Advantage Publishers Group
5880 Oberlin Drive, San Diego, CA 92121-4794
www.thunderbaybooks.com

Copyright © 2004 White Star S.r.l.

Translation: Studio Traduzioni Vecchia, Milan

Printed in China
1 2 3 4 5 08 07 06 05 04

Library of Congress Cataloging-in-Publication Data

Bennet, Guy-Pierre.
  Paris / Guy-Pierre Bennet.
    p. cm.
  ISBN 1-59223-296-5
  1. Paris (France)--Description and travel.
  2. Paris (France)--Social life and customs.
  I. Title.
DC707.B495 2004
944'.361--dc22
                              2004008129